MARLENA SPIELER
THE
CLASSIC
BARBECUE
AND
GRILL
COOKBOOK

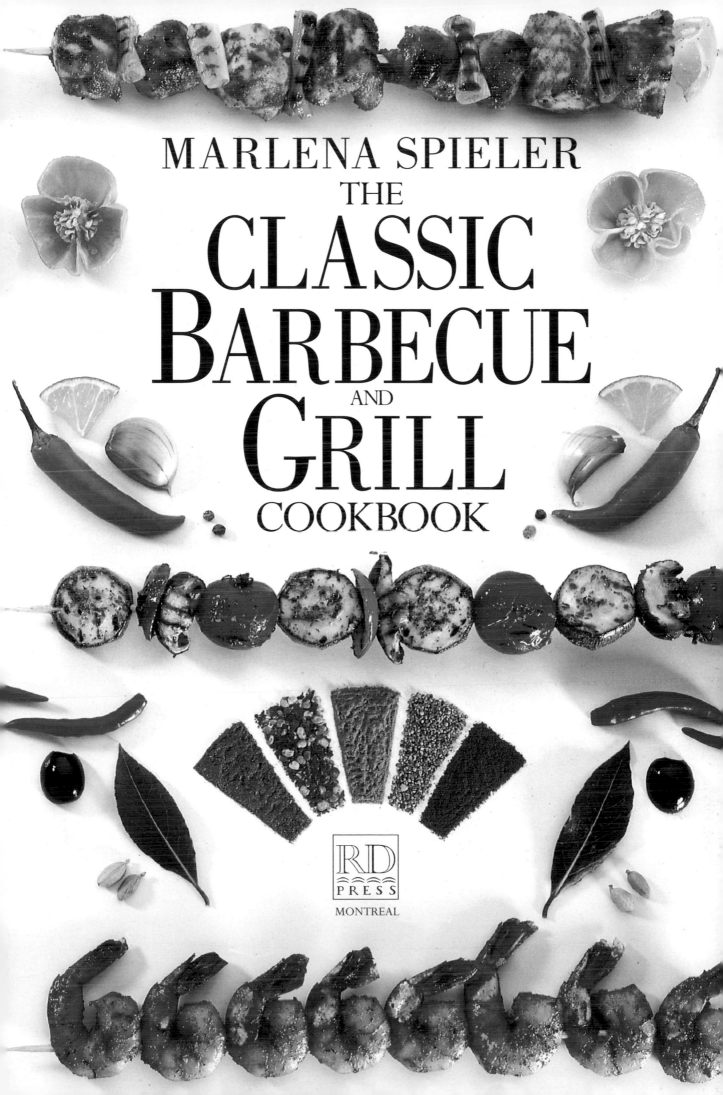

MARLENA SPIELER

THE
CLASSIC
BARBECUE
AND
GRILL
COOKBOOK

RD
PRESS

MONTREAL

A DORLING KINDERSLEY BOOK

Project Editor
Alexa Stace

Art Editor
Kate Scott

Assistant Designer
Emy Manby

Senior Editor
Carolyn Ryden

Senior Art Editor
Vanessa Courtier

Managing Editor
Susannah Marriott

Senior Managing Art Editor
Carole Ash

DTP Designer
Karen Ruane

Photography
Dave King

Production
Maryann Rogers
Manjit Sihra

Published in Canada in 1996 by
The Reader's Digest Association (Canada) Ltd.
215 Redfern Avenue, Westmount, Quebec H3Z 2V9

The Reader's Digest Association (Canada) Ltd
is a licensed user of the trademark RD Press

Canadian Cataloguing in Publication Data

Spieler, Marlena
The classic barbecue and grill cookbook
Includes index.
ISBN 0-88850-513 2
1. Barbecue cookery.   I. Title.
TX840.B3S64 1996   641.5'784   C95-900638-9

Reproduced in Nottingham by Euro Scan
Printed and bound in Italy by A. Mondadori. Verona
96 97 98 99 / 5 4 3 2 1

CONTENTS
INTRODUCTION 6

CLASSIC DISHES 8
*A photographic introduction to ten
classic barbecue dishes and their ingredients*

MARINADES, RUBS & FLAVORINGS 30
*A selection of piquant marinades, spicy dry
rubs and fragrant butters, oils and vinegars*

INTRODUCTION

The appeal of barbecuing is enormous. Before you even taste a morsel you have been teased mercilessly by the delicious aromas that waft from the coals.

Barbecuing was the first cooking technique invented: early hunters would gather around a fire roasting hunks of freshly caught meat. Even today, with sophisticated barbecues and complex recipes, barbecuing remains essentially the same: cooking over fire.

Most of the happy occasions of my life have been accompanied by barbecues. My recent wedding feast, held in a Sonoma County vineyard, featured juicy Tuscan chicken cooked over an open fire, an array of summer vegetables, and bowls of pungent aïoli. When my daughter celebrated her bat mitzvah, we set up a huge barbecue and roasted a wide variety of delicacies for the party.

On travels, the meals I have most enjoyed have often been cooked over open fires. On a recent trip to France we ate a fireside feast of *cargolade* – snails and sausages, served with a garlicky sauce – in Perpignan. Near Cinque Terre I rigged up an impromptu barbecue on the beach and cooked the fish we had caught. One warm evening in a Languedoc cafe I nibbled merguez sausage cooked over grape vine cuttings, a scruffy yet hopeful assortment of dogs at my feet.

Whenever I've found myself snacking on street food, it has usually been cooked over hot coals. In Bulgaria, I have eaten roasted meat tucked into fat bread rolls along with crunchy salads, an Eastern European version of the souvlakia I have so often devoured in Greece. In Mexico, I have frequently been seduced by the promise of smoky-scented meat and fish wrapped up in a tortilla – and who could resist the scent of spicy roasting birds in Thailand?

Though fire-roasted foods are perfect for entertaining, they do not need a special occasion; and though they are eaten all over the world, you do not need a passport to enjoy them. For delectable, memorable barbecuing and grilling, simply light the fire.

A few words about terminology: while barbecuing and grilling both take place over hot coals, there are some major differences. Cooking quickly over direct heat on an uncovered grill or barbecue is *grilling*: this results in meat, fish, poultry or vegetables that are succulent, the juices sealed in from the heat of the fire. Properly, the term *barbecuing* refers to long, slow cooking, covered, over smoldering hardwood. It is thought that the word derives from the Caribbean and Mexican term *barbacoa,* which describes the method of pit-cooking a whole goat, from the tip of its beard to the end of its tail. Traditionally, larger, fattier cuts of meat are barbecued, emerging from the fire permeated with smoky essence, crusty on the outside, well done yet tender and moist within.

I would like to dedicate this book to Gretchen Spieler, who although she may not realize it, taught me how to barbecue in her backyard.

CLASSIC DISHES

From a medley of kebabs that includes lamb brochettes, chicken tikka and curaçao-soaked fruits, to universal favorites such as juicy hamburgers, chargrilled vegetables, and herb-scented fish, the following selection of dishes features foods that are most popularly cooked on barbecues the world over. Middle Eastern flavors dominate in a dish of cumin-encrusted lamb, while herb-scented Tuscan chicken evokes the Mediterranean. For added fire there are spicy Thai-style shrimp and a Mexican feast of shredded beef and chicken fajitas, piled into floury tortillas and served with fiery salsas.

All recipes serve 4 unless otherwise stated.

CHARGRILLED VEGETABLES

A selection of seasonal vegetables, bathed in a garlicky marinade, then barbecued over hot coals, makes a lyrical feast. Tougher vegetables such as artichokes or potatoes need parboiling first, to soften them before they go on the barbecue.

INGREDIENTS

2 medium-sized artichokes, halved and choke removed (see page 152)
4 garlic bulbs
8 large tomatoes, halved
2 fennel bulbs, halved or quartered
½lb (250g) asparagus, ends trimmed
4 scallions, trimmed
2 zucchini, sliced lengthwise
2 ears of corn, cut into bite-sized lengths
8 baby pattypan squash, halved
3 bell peppers, green, red, and yellow, cored, seeded, and cut into thick strips or quarters
2–3 tbsp chopped mixed fresh herbs, such as basil, parsley, oregano, rosemary, thyme, savory, or marjoram

Garlic Marinade
¾ cup (175ml) olive oil
¼ cup (60ml) lemon juice or white. vinegar
salt and black pepper
4–6 garlic cloves, finely chopped
1–2 tbsp chopped fresh rosemary, or 1 tsp dried herbs, such as herbes de Provence

PREPARATION

1 Parboil the artichokes for 8–10 minutes, then drain upside down in a colander.
2 Blanch the garlic bulbs in boiling water for 5–8 minutes, then drain.
3 To make the marinade, place the olive oil, lemon juice, salt and pepper, garlic, and herbs in a bowl and mix well. Place the artichokes in a shallow dish and pour on about ¼ cup (60 ml) of this marinade.
4 Place the vegetables in large bowls and divide the remaining marinade between them. Turn to coat and let marinate for 1½ hours.
5 Prepare a charcoal fire or preheat a gas grill.
6 Drain the vegetables, reserving the marinade. Cook the vegetables in batches over hot coals, turning them once, until just tender inside and chargrilled on the outside. Remove them to a platter as they are ready and sprinkle with the reserved marinade.
7 Serve sprinkled with the chopped fresh herbs, and accompanied by Bruschetta (see page 113) and Red Chili Aïoli (see page 124).

Mixed fresh herbs

Green, red, and yellow bell peppers

Pattypan squash

Garlic

Tomatoes

Asparagus

Scallions

Zucchini

Artichokes

Fennel

Corn on the cob

Lemon juice

Salt

Black pepper

Garlic

Rosemary

Olive oil

MEDITERRANEAN FISH

These barbecued fish remind me of the first time I went to Italy: we arrived in a little fishing village on the northeast coast and immediately stopped at the market for provisions. A cache of small fish went into my bag, along with fennel, peppers, garlic, and parsley. We rigged up a primitive barbecue on the beach and cooked the fish, serving them with a salad of fennel and red peppers, and with chunks of bread to scoop it all up.

INGREDIENTS

2lb (1kg) sardines, sprats, or whitebait,
with heads still on, cleaned only if they are
larger than 4–5in (10–12cm)
3 garlic cloves, finely chopped
juice of ½ lemon
2 tbsp Pernod, ouzo, or
other anise-flavored alcohol
3 tbsp olive oil
2 tbsp chopped fresh parsley
salt and black pepper
lemon wedges, to garnish

PREPARATION

1 Place the fish in a large shallow dish and add the garlic, lemon juice, Pernod, olive oil, and half the parsley. Turn to coat well, then marinate for 30–60 minutes at room temperature.
2 Prepare a charcoal fire or preheat a gas grill.
3 Drain the fish and cook over hot coals for approximately 3–4 minutes on each side, until they develop grill marks and are just cooked through. If cooked covered, they may not need turning.
4 Season well, then serve immediately, garnished with wedges of lemon and sprinkled with the remaining parsley. Accompany with a salad of fennel and peppers.

VARIATIONS

SNAPPER, BASS, OR TILAPIA Larger fish, 2–3 lb (1–1.5 kg), can also be cooked very successfully in this way. Cut 2–3 deep diagonal slashes on both sides of the fish, so that the marinade flavors can permeate the flesh. Cook for 20–25 minutes on each side, until cooked through, using a wire grill basket if you have one.
GRILLED FISH WITH MOROCCAN FLAVORS Omit the Pernod and double the amount of lemon juice. Substitute fresh cilantro for half the parsley and add a large pinch each of curry powder, ground cumin, and turmeric to the marinade.

Olive oil

Lemon juice

Pernod

Garlic

Sardines

Parsley

Salt

Black pepper

Lemon wedges

GRILLED SALMON WITH LEEKS

Salmon is an ideal fish to barbecue. Its slightly oily texture holds up well even in the heat of the fire, and its distinctive flavor combines well with the smoky scent of the barbecue. The lemony chive and watercress butter makes a tangy fresh sauce as it melts onto the fish. Chargrilled baby leeks are a marvelous accompaniment; if they are not available, use ordinary-sized leeks, or raw scallions tossed with olive oil and vinegar before barbecuing.

INGREDIENTS

8 baby leeks, cleaned and trimmed
4 x 1in (2.5cm) thick salmon steaks,
about ½lb (250g) each
3 tbsp olive oil or melted butter
salt and black pepper
Chive, Lemon, & Watercress Butter
4 tbsp butter, softened
1 garlic clove, finely chopped
1 shallot, finely chopped
2 tbsp chopped chives
1 small bunch watercress, chopped
juice of ½ lemon
salt and black pepper

PREPARATION

1 Prepare a charcoal fire or preheat a gas grill.
2 Meanwhile, make the flavored butter. Combine the butter with the garlic, shallot, chives, and watercress, then blend in the lemon juice and seasoning. Drain off any excess liquid and form the butter into a sausage shape. Wrap in plastic wrap and chill until firm.
3 Blanch the leeks in boiling water for about 2 minutes, then drain, refresh under cold running water, and drain well again.
4 Brush the salmon and the leeks with oil or melted butter. Sprinkle with salt and pepper.
5 Place the fish and leeks on the barbecue over medium-hot coals and cook for 3–5 minutes on each side, until the salmon is fairly firm and the leeks have marks from the grill.
6 Serve immediately, with a nugget of the chilled butter on top of each salmon steak.

VARIATION

GRILLED STEAKS WITH LEEKS Tender lean beef is delicious with melting Chive, Lemon, & Watercress Butter. Adjust the cooking time to 4–5 minutes so that the meat remains rare and juicy.

Butter

Black pepper

Salt

Olive oil

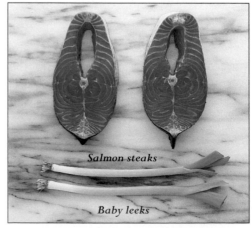

Salmon steaks

Baby leeks

Garlic

Shallot

Chives

Watercress

Lemon juice

THAI-STYLE SHRIMP

A hot, spicy marinade and coconut-flavored sauce give these shrimp the authentic flavor of Thailand. Serve with Southeast Asian Noodle Salad (see page 134) or crisp raw bean sprouts. Halve the quantity of marinade if serving shrimp as an appetizer.

INGREDIENTS

raw tiger shrimp in their shells, heads removed,
or large shrimp, 12 as an appetizer or
24 for a main dish
walnut-sized piece of creamed coconut
blended with ¼ cup (60ml) water, or
¼ cup (60ml) unsweetened coconut milk
chili flowers (see page 153), to garnish

Thai Marinade

¼ red pepper, cored, seeded,
and finely chopped
4 garlic cloves, finely chopped
2 tbsp chopped fresh cilantro
2 tbsp vinegar
juice of 2 limes
1 stalk lemongrass, finely chopped,
or zest of ¼ lemon
½ tsp turmeric, or to taste
¼ cup (60ml) vegetable oil
pinch of ground cumin
1–2 green chilies, finely chopped
½ tsp crushed dried red chilies,
or red chili paste
1 tsp sugar, or to taste

PREPARATION

1 Prepare a charcoal fire or preheat a gas grill.
2 Combine the marinade ingredients in a bowl. Place the tiger shrimp in a shallow dish and pour over the marinade. Turn until well coated, then refrigerate for 30 minutes.
3 Get 4 or 8 skewers ready – wooden skewers should be soaked in cold water for 30 minutes.
4 Drain the shrimp, reserving the marinade. Thread 3 or 4 shrimp on each skewer, piercing each shrimp twice. Cook over medium-hot to hot coals, 2–3 minutes on each side, basting once or twice, until the shrimp are pink.
5 Meanwhile, pour the marinade into a small pan, stir in the coconut milk, and heat over the grill until the sauce thickens, about 5 minutes.
6 To serve, arrange some Southeast Asian Noodle Salad (see page 134) on each plate with the shrimp on skewers. Pour over the hot sauce, and garnish with a chili flower (see page 153).

Lemongrass

Lime juice

Cilantro

Vinegar

Garlic

Red pepper

Creamed coconut

Tiger shrimp

Turmeric

Vegetable oil

Ground
cumin

Green
chilies

Crushed red
chilies

Sugar

Chili
flower

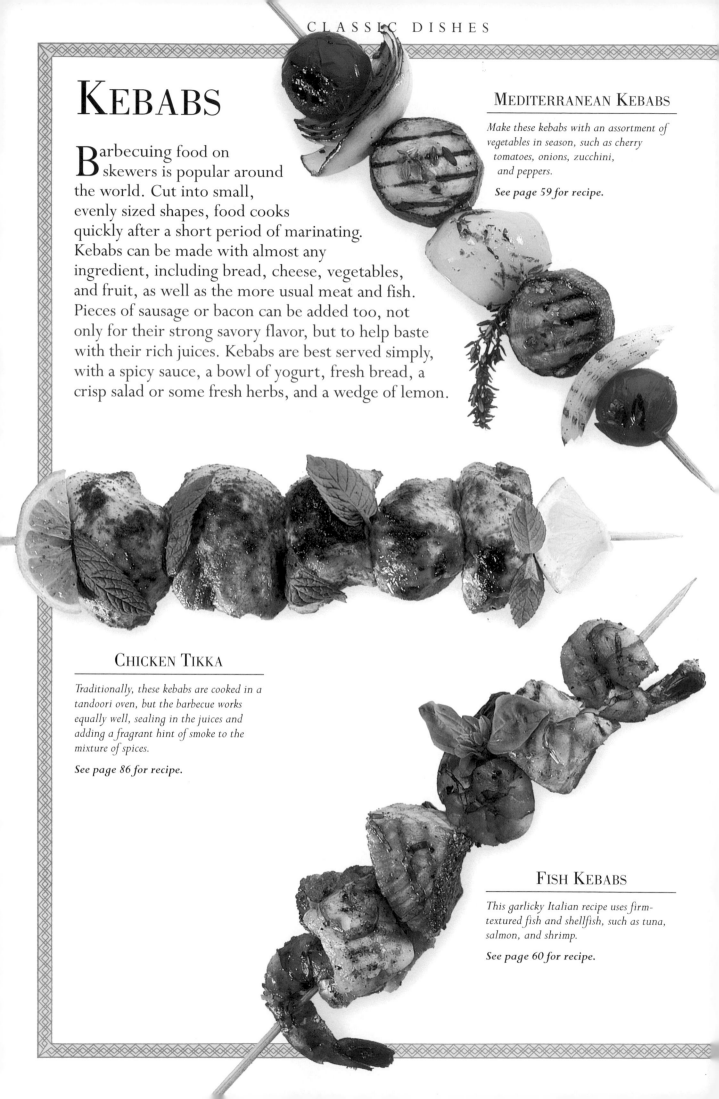

KEBABS

Barbecuing food on skewers is popular around the world. Cut into small, evenly sized shapes, food cooks quickly after a short period of marinating. Kebabs can be made with almost any ingredient, including bread, cheese, vegetables, and fruit, as well as the more usual meat and fish. Pieces of sausage or bacon can be added too, not only for their strong savory flavor, but to help baste with their rich juices. Kebabs are best served simply, with a spicy sauce, a bowl of yogurt, fresh bread, a crisp salad or some fresh herbs, and a wedge of lemon.

MEDITERRANEAN KEBABS

Make these kebabs with an assortment of vegetables in season, such as cherry tomatoes, onions, zucchini, and peppers.

See page 59 for recipe.

CHICKEN TIKKA

Traditionally, these kebabs are cooked in a tandoori oven, but the barbecue works equally well, sealing in the juices and adding a fragrant hint of smoke to the mixture of spices.

See page 86 for recipe.

FISH KEBABS

This garlicky Italian recipe uses firm-textured fish and shellfish, such as tuna, salmon, and shrimp.

See page 60 for recipe.

HALLOUMI, TOMATO, & BAY LEAF KEBABS

Serve these kebabs with crusty bread for an ideal snack or on their own as a wonderful appetizer.

See page 119 for recipe.

CURAÇAO FRUIT KEBABS

Almost any fruit can be cooked on the barbecue. These peach, banana, and apricot kebabs are hot and smoky, yet sweet. Serve with vanilla ice cream.

See page 122 for recipe.

MOROCCAN LAMB BROCHETTES

Serve these brochettes hot off the grill, sprinkled with paprika and freshly chopped cilantro.

See page 98 for recipe.

TUSCAN CHICKEN

Amarinade of olive oil and lemon juice, combined with garlic and sprigs
of fresh rosemary, is perfect for flavoring chicken to produce a
classic Tuscan taste. I like to add a selection of vegetables – here
peppers, zucchini, and asparagus – but you can use whatever
is in season. Good-quality herbed chicken sausages would also
make an enticing addition to the feast. Serve the chicken
with Aïoli (see page 66) and a sprinkling of black olives.

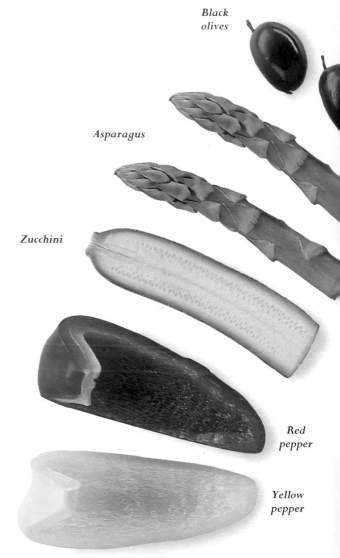

Black
olives

Asparagus

Zucchini

Red
pepper

Yellow
pepper

INGREDIENTS

1 chicken, about 3lb (1.5kg), cut into 8 pieces
1 yellow and 1 red pepper, cored,
seeded, and cut into wedges
4 small zucchini, sliced lengthwise
1lb (500g) asparagus, ends trimmed
handful of black olives, to garnish
Tuscan Marinade
10 garlic cloves, finely chopped
juice of 3 lemons
2–3 tbsp chopped fresh rosemary
salt and black pepper
⅓ cup (90ml) olive oil

PREPARATION

1 To make the marinade, combine the garlic,
lemon juice, rosemary, a pinch of salt, some black
pepper, and the olive oil in a small bowl and blend
the mixture well.
2 Place the chicken pieces in a large shallow dish.
Pour two thirds of the marinade over the chicken,
reserving the remainder to baste the vegetables.
Cover the chicken and refrigerate for at least 2
hours (overnight, or even for 2 nights, is ideal).
3 Prepare a charcoal fire or preheat a gas grill.
4 When the coals are medium-hot, arrange the
chicken on the grill, adding dark meat first and
breast meat last. Move the pieces around so that
they cook evenly. If the barbecue has a lid, cover
the chicken pieces.
5 When the chicken is almost done (approximately
8–10 minutes for white meat and 20 minutes for
dark meat, or until the juices run clear when the
flesh is pierced with a skewer), toss the peppers,
zucchini, and asparagus in half the remaining
marinade. Place the vegetables on the grill and
cook for about 2 minutes on each side, basting
them with the rest of the marinade.
6 To serve, pile the vegetables around the chicken
pieces. Garnish with black olives and serve
accompanied by Aïoli (see page 66).

Chicken

Garlic

Lemon
juice

Rosemary

Salt

Black
pepper

Olive oil

CUMIN ROAST LAMB

Cumin paste gives a rustic, Middle Eastern scent to food – it's also good with fish, such as snapper, cod, or halibut. To serve this dish, I like to pile the grilled meat and vegetables around a central platter of pilaf (see page 133) to create a communal feast. Leave the pumpkin unpeeled: the skin helps it keep its shape and is easily removed after cooking.

Olive oil

Eggplant

Pumpkin

INGREDIENTS

4 baby leeks or small brown onions, or 8 scallions
1lb (500g) pumpkin or other orange winter squash,
cut into ¼in (5mm) slices, unpeeled
1 eggplant, cut into wedges or thick slices
2 tbsp olive oil
juice of ½ lemon
4 lamb steaks, 6–8oz (175–250g) each
cilantro leaves, to garnish
Cumin Paste
2 tbsp cumin seeds
2 tbsp ground cumin
6 garlic cloves, crushed
1 tsp salt
¼ cup (60ml) olive oil
2 tbsp chopped fresh cilantro or parsley
juice of 1 lemon

PREPARATION

1 Place the cumin paste ingredients in a bowl and mix together well.
2 Blanch the leeks for 1–2 minutes in boiling water, then drain well. Place in a shallow dish with the pumpkin and eggplant.
3 Drizzle the vegetables with the olive oil and lemon juice, then sprinkle on 1–2 tablespoons of the cumin paste and turn to coat well.
4 Place the lamb steaks in a shallow dish and sprinkle on the remaining cumin paste, turning to coat well on all sides. Let the lamb and vegetables marinate for at least 30 minutes.
5 Meanwhile, prepare a charcoal fire or preheat a gas grill.
6 Place the meat and vegetables on the barbecue over hot coals. Turn everything once or twice while cooking, so that the lamb is browned on the outside but still pink inside, and the vegetables are tender, with grill marks.
7 Serve the lamb and vegetables with Middle Eastern Spiced Pilaf (see page 133) and garnish with cilantro leaves. Accompany with Cucumber-Yogurt Relish (see page 129), if desired.

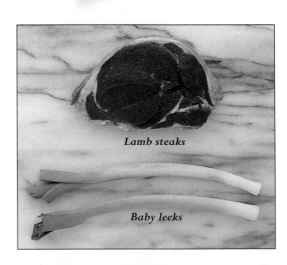

Lamb steaks

Baby leeks

Lemon juice

Cumin
seeds

Ground
cumin

Garlic

Salt

Cilantro

ALL-AMERICAN RIBS

Barbecued ribs are delicious rubbed with a dry spice mixture, then basted, or "mopped," as they cook on the barbecue. The secret of their flavor is long, slow cooking, the ribs growing tender and smoky as they cook on the fire. Brush sweet and spicy She-Devil Barbecue Sauce (see page 127) on the ribs during the last 10 minutes of cooking, and offer an extra bowlful at the table.

Garlic powder

Dry mustard

INGREDIENTS

2lb (1kg) pork spareribs, either
in a sheet or separated
4 leeks, cut into brushes
(see page 152), for basting
Down-Home Dry Rub
1 tbsp onion powder
1 tbsp salt
1 tsp black pepper
3 tbsp paprika
1 tbsp dry mustard
1 tbsp garlic powder
1 tbsp crumbled dried bay leaves
Lone Star Moppin' Sauce
⅔ cup (150ml) cider vinegar
⅓ cup (90ml) vegetable oil
¼ cup (60ml) Worcestershire sauce
½ tsp Tabasco or other hot sauce
1 tbsp paprika
1 tbsp mild chili powder
1 tsp dry mustard
1 tsp crumbled dried bay leaves
1 tsp garlic powder
½ tsp celery salt, or to taste

Paprika

Black pepper

Salt

PREPARATION

1 Mix the dry rub ingredients together in a bowl. Dust the ribs with the dry rub, then rub it in well. Let marinate for 30 minutes.
2 Prepare a charcoal fire or preheat a gas grill.
3 To make the Lone Star Moppin' Sauce, place all the ingredients in a bowl and mix together well.
4 Cook the ribs on a cool part of the grill, basting with the Moppin' Sauce, using a leek brush. Keep covered, so that the smoke scents the meat. The longer and slower the ribs cook, the more tender they will be. Allow 1–2 hours if the ribs are in a sheet, about 40 minutes if separated. To cook over medium heat, halve the cooking time.
5 Brush with She-Devil Barbecue Sauce (see page 127) when the ribs are almost done. Serve immediately, passing around the remaining sauce.

Onion powder

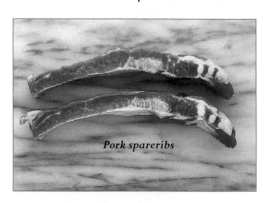

Pork spareribs

Vegetable oil

Tabasco sauce

Cider vinegar

Worcestershire
sauce

Mild chili
powder

Celery salt

Bay leaves

FAJITAS

A Mexican feast, fajitas consist of various kinds of meat, such as chicken, beef, and sometimes sausage, marinated in a spicy chili paste, then barbecued with plantains and onions until crusty and smoky flavored. Traditionally, the meats are then shredded and served in flour tortillas or crisp corn tacos accompanied by guacamole, refried beans, sour cream, and salsa. The contrasts between the smoky meats, spicy salsa, soft tortillas, earthy beans, and tangy cream are superb. See page 99 for the Fajitas recipe.

SHREDDED BEEF

Thinly sliced or shredded beef is perfect for tortilla fillings.
See page 99 for recipe.

SALSA

Quick to prepare, Salsa can be puréed for a smoother texture.
See page 124 for recipe.

SOUR CREAM

Serve this tangy cream sprinkled with paprika, as a cooling accompaniment to spicy dishes.

REFRIED BEANS

Spicy puréed pinto beans.
See page 132 for recipe.

GUACAMOLE

Avocado dip is one of the traditional side dishes.
See page 126 for recipe.

PLANTAINS & ONIONS

Barbecued onions and slices of plantain add an intense burst of flavor.
See page 99 for recipe.

FAJITAS

Traditionally, fajitas are served in a flour tortilla.
See page 99 for recipe.

SHREDDED CHICKEN

Chicken is first spread with Chili & Tequila Paste.
See page 99 for recipe.

BURGERS

What springs to mind when you think of a burger? A juicy meat patty, cooked over a charcoal fire, stuffed into a plump bun, and slathered with piquant relishes. This sandwich got its name at the turn of the century, when sailors from Hamburg, Germany, docked in New York. Snacking on charcoal-grilled burgers sold by street vendors, some sailors had the idea of tucking them into bread rolls to carry back to their ship. The public first encountered this sandwich at the World's Fair in 1903–4 in St. Louis, and it became an instant classic.

INGREDIENTS

1½lb (750g) lean ground beef
8 shallots or 1 onion, finely chopped
3–4 tbsp heavy cream
4 small flat ice cubes, optional
salt and black pepper
4 sesame buns
sliced tomato, onion, and dill pickles, to garnish
Shredded Lettuce Burger Sauce
½ cup (125g) mayonnaise
3 tbsp Dijon mustard, or a combination of
brown and yellow mustard
½ head iceberg lettuce, or 1 head
green lettuce, shredded
4 shallots, finely chopped
juice of ½ lemon

PREPARATION

1 Prepare a charcoal fire or preheat a gas grill.
2 Place the beef in a large bowl and break it up with a fork. Add the shallots and cream and beat with a wooden spoon until well combined.
3 Using wet hands, shape the mixture into 4 large balls, then flatten them with your fingers to make patties about 1in (2.5cm) thick. Insert a small ice cube in the center of each patty to keep the meat moist, if desired.
4 Generously sprinkle the patties with salt and pepper and place on the barbecue over hot coals. Cook for 3 minutes, then turn to cook the other side. Continue until the meat is done to taste.
5 To make the sauce, blend the mayonnaise and mustard together in a bowl. Add the lettuce and shallots and toss until well combined. Season with lemon juice to taste.
6 Split the sesame buns in half and toast on the barbecue. Serve each burger in a bun, topped with the sauce. Garnish with sliced tomato, onion rings, and dill pickles.

Salt

Ice cubes

Heavy cream

Shallots

Ground beef

Sesame buns

Dill pickle

Mayonnaise

Black pepper

Dijon mustard

Lettuce

Lemon juice

Tomato

Onion rings

MARINADES, RUBS, & FLAVORINGS

*Bathing food in an aromatic marinade helps
tenderize and add succulence while protecting
it from the heat of the fire. Hot spices, pungent
sauces, and zesty citrus juices all imbue foods with
distinct tastes. Some marinades form glazes, while dry
rubs add piquancy. To add character to marinades,
steep your favorite herbs and spices in oils and
vinegars. Serve flavored butters on top of
the cooked food for an extra smooth, rich finish.*

MARINADES

A simple marinade can transform food for the barbecue, whether it is meat, fish, poultry, or vegetables. Besides enhancing the flavor, a marinade helps to prevent moisture loss. Acidic marinades containing wine, vinegar, mustard, or citrus juice penetrate and tenderize food. Oil and paste marinades form a savory crust that seals in moisture, while dry herb and spice marinades are rubbed into food just before cooking.

TIMING & PREPARATION

◆ Red meat, poultry, and game (whole and cut up) are usually marinated for up to 2 hours at room temperature or up to 48 hours in the refrigerator.
◆ Whole fish, fillets, and steaks and seafood can be marinated for up to 30 minutes at room temperature, or up to 2 hours in the refrigerator.
◆ Vegetables and tofu can be marinated for up to 30 minutes at room temperature, or up to 2 hours in the refrigerator – overnight for tofu.
◆ Bring refrigerated food back to room temperature before cooking, and brush off excess marinade.

Garlic

Chili paste

Paprika

Ground cumin

Oregano

Beer

SPICY MEXICAN MARINADE

This spicy marinade gives a rich red coating. Sufficient for 2lb (1kg) lean meat or fish.

INGREDIENTS

*3 garlic cloves, finely chopped
1 tbsp chili powder, lightly toasted and mixed to a paste with water
1 tbsp paprika
1 tsp ground cumin
$\frac{1}{2}$ tsp dried oregano
2 tbsp beer or tequila
juice of 1 orange and 1 lime, or
3 tbsp pineapple juice
2 tbsp olive oil
2 tbsp chopped fresh cilantro
coarsely ground salt, to taste*

PREPARATION

Combine the ingredients in a shallow dish. Add the food, turn to coat, and marinate (see above for timing).

Orange and lime juice

Olive oil

Cilantro

Salt

Rosemary

Fennel
seeds

Black
pepper

Salt

Sage

Oregano

Parsley

Olive oil

Lemon and
juice

Garlic

LEMON-HERB MARINADE

*Sufficient for 2lb (1kg) chicken, pork,
or fish, or 1½lb (750g) vegetables.*

INGREDIENTS

*3 garlic cloves, finely chopped
1 lemon, thinly sliced
juice of 1 lemon
3 tbsp olive oil
½ cup finely chopped mixed fresh parsley,
oregano, sage, and rosemary
1 tsp fennel seeds
black pepper and coarsely ground salt, to taste*

PREPARATION

Combine the ingredients in a dish. Add the
food and marinate (see page 32 for timing).

SOUTH SEAS COCONUT MARINADE

This marinade is finished off with an apricot glaze.
Enough to marinate 1lb (500g) fish fillets.

INGREDIENTS

1 tbsp curry powder
1 tbsp soy sauce or fish sauce
½ cup (125ml) coconut milk
juice of 1 lime
2 tbsp apricot jam or chutney
ground cayenne, to taste

PREPARATION

1 Combine the curry powder, soy sauce, coconut milk, and half the lime juice. Pour over the fish and let marinate (see page 32 for timing).
2 Mix the remaining lime juice with the jam and cayenne. Brush the fish with this glaze during the last few minutes of cooking.

AFRO-CAJUN MARINADE

For crisp, spicy chicken wings; enough for 2lb (1kg).

INGREDIENTS

juice of 2–3 lemons
1 onion, grated
6 garlic cloves, finely chopped
½ tsp ground cumin
1 tbsp syrup from a jar of preserved ginger
¼ tsp ground cinnamon
pinch of ground cloves
¼ tsp ground cayenne, or to taste
1 tbsp vegetable or olive oil

PREPARATION

Combine the ingredients in a dish, toss the chicken to coat well, and marinate (see page 32 for timing).

SWEET-SPICY MUSTARD MARINADE

Marvelous for tiny kebabs, chicken wings, shrimp,
or lamb chops. Enough to coat 1½lb (750g).

INGREDIENTS

3 tbsp apricot jam or marmalade
1 tbsp Dijon mustard
2 tbsp honey
1 tbsp brown sugar
1 tbsp cider vinegar
1 tbsp sesame oil

PREPARATION

Combine the ingredients in a shallow dish, toss the food to coat well, and cook quickly over a high heat – the sugar will char with long cooking.

GREEN MASALA MARINADE

Perfect for lamb chops or cutlets; enough to coat 2lb (1kg).

INGREDIENTS

1 bulb garlic, cloves separated and finely chopped
3 tbsp lemon juice
3 tbsp plain yogurt
1 tsp ground cumin
1 tsp turmeric
1 tsp ground coriander
1 tsp garam masala
1 tbsp finely chopped fresh mint leaves
1 tbsp finely chopped fresh cilantro leaves
5 cardamom pods, hulls removed and seeds crushed
⅔ cup (150ml) olive oil
salt and ground cayenne, to taste

PREPARATION

Mix the marinade in a shallow dish, add the meat, and marinate (see page 32 for timing).

Afro-Cajun Marinade

Green Masala Marinade

TIKKA MASALA MARINADE

Ideal for giving an authentic, spicy Indian flavor to bland foods such as tofu or chicken pieces. Enough for 2lb (1kg) chicken pieces or 10oz (300g) tofu.

INGREDIENTS

2 garlic cloves, finely chopped
1 tsp chopped fresh ginger
2 tbsp plain yogurt
pinch of ground cayenne
2–3 tsp cumin seeds
pinch of turmeric
1 tbsp tandoori or tikka paste
2 tbsp chopped fresh cilantro

PREPARATION

Combine the ingredients well in a shallow dish. Add the tofu or chicken and turn to coat well. Let marinate (see page 32 for timing).

TERIYAKI MARINADE

This Japanese-style marinade is enough to coat 2lb (1kg) fish, poultry, or meat.

INGREDIENTS

¼ cup (60ml) soy sauce
¼ cup (60ml) sesame oil
¼ cup (60ml) rice wine or dry sherry
2 tbsp sugar
2 scallions, thinly sliced
2 garlic cloves, chopped
1 tsp grated fresh ginger

PREPARATION

Combine the ingredients in a shallow dish, add the food, turn to coat well, and marinate (see page 32 for timing).

HOISIN MARINADE

A classic Chinese sauce; enough for 1½lb (750g) chops.

INGREDIENTS

1 cup (250ml) hoisin sauce
2–3 tbsp rice vinegar
2 tbsp soy sauce
5 garlic cloves, finely chopped
pinch of five-spice powder
1 tbsp sugar
2 tbsp sesame oil
dash of Tabasco or other hot sauce

PREPARATION

Combine the ingredients, turn the chops to coat well, and marinate (see page 32 for timing).

BASIC YOGURT MARINADE

Suitable for 2lb (1kg) chicken, lamb, or fish.

INGREDIENTS

1 cup (250g) plain yogurt
2–3 garlic cloves, finely chopped
1 onion, finely chopped or grated
½ tsp ground cinnamon
½ tsp ground cumin
½ tsp crushed black peppercorns
¼ tsp ground ginger
¼ tsp cloves
¼ tsp nutmeg
¼ tsp ground cayenne
2 cardamom pods, hulls removed and seeds crushed
1 tsp salt

PREPARATION

Combine well, add the food, and marinate (see page 32 for timing).

Teriyaki Marinade

Basic Yogurt Marinade

Garlic

Scallions

Dark
brown
sugar

Lemon zest
and juice

Chilies

Soy
sauce

Turmeric

Ground
coriander

Fresh
ginger

Peanuts

INDONESIAN MARINADE

*Enough for 4 small Cornish hens or
3½lb (1.75kg) chicken pieces.*

INGREDIENTS

*5–7 garlic cloves, finely chopped
4 scallions or 5 shallots, chopped
4 tbsp dark brown sugar
grated zest and juice of 2 lemons
2–3 green jalapeño chilies,
finely chopped
⅓ cup (90ml) soy sauce
½ tsp turmeric
1 tbsp ground coriander
3 tbsp finely chopped fresh ginger
1 cup (100g) peanuts, ground or finely chopped*

PREPARATION

Mix the ingredients in a shallow dish. Add the
chicken pieces, turn to coat well, and marinate for
3–4 hours at room temperature, or up to 48 hours
in the refrigerator.

Bay
leaves

Herbes de
Provence

Salt

Black
pepper

Garlic

Onions

Sugar

Red wine

Grenadine

INGREDIENTS

½ cup (125ml) grenadine
¼ cup (60ml) red wine
2 tbsp sugar
2 onions, grated
5 garlic cloves, coarsely chopped
5–8 fresh bay leaves
2 tsp herbes de Provence
salt and black pepper

PREPARATION

Combine the ingredients in a large shallow dish.
Add the duck, or lamb chops, and turn to coat
well. Cover and marinate for 3–4 hours at room
temperature, or up to 48 hours in the refrigerator.

POMEGRANATE & WINE MARINADE

*This tangy-sweet marinade is ideal for rich lamb or
duck. It is enough for 2 medium-sized ducks,
cut into serving pieces, or 2lb (1kg) lamb chops.*

Olive oil

Red wine

Shallots

Garlic

Fresh herbs

Salt

Black pepper

BASIC WINE MARINADE

This basic marinade can be varied to taste. In general, red meat such as beef, duck, or lamb will require a red wine marinade, chicken and fish a white one, but I have marinated chicken breasts in red wine with delicious results. Makes enough for 2lb (1kg) meat, poultry, or fish.

INGREDIENTS

¼ cup (60ml) olive oil
¼ cup (60ml) red or white wine
2 shallots, finely chopped, or 1 onion, grated
2 garlic cloves, finely chopped, optional
1 tbsp chopped fresh herbs
salt and black pepper

PREPARATION

Combine the ingredients in a shallow dish.
Add meat or fish of choice, turn to coat well, and
marinate (see page 32 for timing).

Black pepper

Fresh ginger

Ground allspice

Thyme

Onions

Chilies

Garlic

Tarragon vinegar

Soy sauce

White wine

JAMAICAN JERK

Throughout Jamaica "jerk" seasoning is used for marinating meats that are then roasted over an open fire until brown, crusty, and spicy hot. Makes enough to marinate 2lb (1kg) beef, pork, or chicken.

INGREDIENTS

¼ cup (60ml) white or red wine
2 tbsp tarragon vinegar
2 tbsp soy sauce
5–8 garlic cloves, finely chopped
1–2 Scotch bonnet chilies, finely chopped
2 onions, finely chopped
1 tsp black pepper
1 tbsp finely chopped fresh ginger
1 tsp ground allspice
1 tsp dried thyme

PREPARATION

Combine the ingredients in a shallow dish and toss the meat in the mixture to coat well. Marinate (see page 32 for timing).

DRY RUBS

Dry rubs are mixtures of spices and herbs that are rubbed into food before cooking. They have no oil to moisten or acids to tenderize; they are all flavor. Use with fatty cuts of meat, or mix with a little oil and wine for a flavoring paste to brush on before grilling. Dry rubs are also good used with basting sauces, such as She-Devil Barbecue Sauce (see page 127). The spice-herb coating gives a lovely crispness to the food and the sauce adds the final touch.

CAJUN SPICE RUB

Makes enough for 2lb (1kg) meat.

INGREDIENTS

2 tbsp paprika
1 tbsp ground cumin
1 tbsp dried thyme
1 tbsp onion powder
1 tbsp garlic powder
1 tbsp dried oregano
1 tsp black pepper
1 tsp ground cayenne

PREPARATION

Rub on food to be barbecued quickly and simply. Serve with a flavored butter (see pages 42–43).

Paprika

Ground cumin

Thyme

Onion powder

Garlic powder

Oregano

Black pepper

Cayenne

PASTES & GLAZES

Aromatic spicy pastes give a great flavor to barbecued food. Because they are thick, pastes tend to stay on the surface and are not absorbed: use for thin, delicate items such as fish fillets or chicken breasts. Glazes are similar to pastes, but sweeter. Chutneys and jams, combined with mustards, vinegar, and sugar, make tasty, tangy glazes. Always brush on a glaze toward the end of cooking, and beware of charring the food, as the sugar quickly caramelizes and burns.

MEXICAN CHILI PASTE

Enough for 1 medium-large or 2 small chickens.

INGREDIENTS

grated zest and juice of 1 orange, 1 lime, and 1 lemon
5 garlic cloves, finely crushed
3 tbsp mild chili powder
1 tbsp paprika
1 tsp ground cumin
½ tsp dried oregano
¼ tsp ground cinnamon
1 tbsp olive oil
1 tsp salt
½ green chili, chopped, or more to taste

PREPARATION

Mix ½ teaspoon of each fruit zest and all the juices with the other ingredients, adding more spices if desired. Let stand for at least 30 minutes to thicken, before coating the meat.

RUM GLAZE

This glaze is excellent with fattier meats since there is no oil in the mixture. Makes enough to glaze 1½lb (750g) chops or steaks.

INGREDIENTS

½ cup (100g) brown sugar
2 tbsp dark rum
juice of 1 lime or 2 tbsp pineapple juice
grated zest of ½ lime
1 tbsp dry mustard

PREPARATION

1 Mix all the ingredients together.
2 Coat the meat with a dry rub and cook over low heat. Brush on the glaze toward the end of the cooking time.

MANGO-MUSTARD GLAZE

A spicy, sweet-hot glaze is just right for barbecued duck pieces as it keeps the skin crisp. Enough for 1 medium-sized duck or 1½lb (750g) chops or kebabs.

INGREDIENTS

2½ tbsp mango chutney
1½ tbsp Dijon mustard
1½ tbsp marmalade or apricot jam
several drops of Tabasco or other hot sauce

PREPARATION

1 Mix all the ingredients together, then brush over the cooked food.
2 Return to the barbecue and continue cooking for 15–20 minutes, or until glazed but not burned.

Mexican Chili Paste

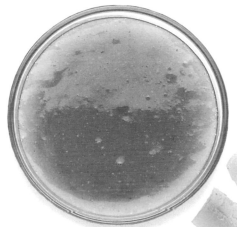

Mango-Mustard Glaze

FLAVORED BUTTERS

Flavored butter makes a rich sauce for simple barbecued food. Serve a slice or two on top of chops, steaks, or fish to melt and combine with the hot juices. For a pouring sauce, warm the flavored butter over the barbecue just before serving. The butters will keep for up to 1 week in the refrigerator, and up to 2 months in the freezer: simply shape into a roll and freeze in plastic wrap.

Cilantro & Green Chili Butter

BASIC SHALLOT BUTTER

INGREDIENTS

½ cup (125g) unsalted butter, softened
dash of lemon juice
2 shallots, finely chopped
salt and black pepper

PREPARATION

Combine all the ingredients well, then either serve at room temperature or chill and slice. Place on the hot food and allow it to melt and blend in.

VARIATIONS

TARRAGON BUTTER Add 2 teaspoons of chopped fresh tarragon to the Basic Shallot Butter.
FRESH DILL BUTTER Dill butter is excellent with grilled salmon. Add 2 teaspoons of chopped fresh dill to the Basic Shallot Butter.

Black Olive & Sage Butter

CILANTRO & GREEN CHILI BUTTER

INGREDIENTS

½ cup (125g) unsalted butter, softened
¼ cup (15g) chopped fresh cilantro
3 scallions, thinly sliced
2 garlic cloves, finely chopped
¼ green chili, or to taste, finely chopped
dash of lime
pinch of grated lime zest
salt, to taste

PREPARATION

Combine the butter with the cilantro, scallions, garlic, chili, and lime juice and zest. Mix well and season to taste with salt.

Raspberry & Roasted Garlic Butter

BLACK OLIVE & SAGE BUTTER

INGREDIENTS

1/2 cup (125g) unsalted butter, softened
8–10 fresh sage leaves, chopped
2–3 tbsp black olives in oil, drained and coarsely chopped
2 garlic cloves, finely chopped

PREPARATION

Combine the butter with the other ingredients. Use with veal or small roast birds.

Rosemary-Mustard Butter

Sun-Dried Tomato & Basil Butter

Green Peppercorn Butter

ROSEMARY-MUSTARD BUTTER

INGREDIENTS

½ cup (125g) unsalted butter, softened
1 tbsp Dijon mustard
2 garlic cloves, finely chopped
2 tbsp chopped fresh rosemary
salt and black pepper

PREPARATION

Combine the butter with the other ingredients and season to taste. Use with veal or lamb chops.

SUN-DRIED TOMATO & BASIL BUTTER

INGREDIENTS

4 garlic cloves, finely chopped
½ cup (125g) unsalted butter, softened
5–8 sun-dried tomatoes in oil, diced, plus ½ tsp of the oil
3 tbsp finely chopped fresh basil leaves
salt and black pepper

PREPARATION

Combine the garlic with the butter and sun-dried tomatoes, then work in the basil and season well.

GREEN PEPPERCORN BUTTER

INGREDIENTS

1 tbsp green peppercorns in water, drained
3 shallots, finely chopped
½ cup (125g) unsalted butter, softened
1 tbsp brandy
salt and black pepper

PREPARATION

Pound the peppercorns using a mortar and pestle or with a fork. Add the shallots, butter, and brandy and mix well. Season to taste.

RASPBERRY & ROASTED GARLIC BUTTER

INGREDIENTS

6 roasted garlic cloves, peeled and puréed (see page 152)
½ cup (125g) unsalted butter, softened
25 fresh raspberries, mashed
dash of raspberry vinegar
salt and black pepper

PREPARATION

Combine the garlic with the butter. Mix well, then work in the raspberries and vinegar, and season.

HAZELNUT BUTTER

INGREDIENTS

½ cup (125g) unsalted butter, softened
3 shallots, chopped
4 tbsp chopped hazelnuts, toasted
1–2 tsp pear, cider, or raspberry vinegar
salt and black pepper

PREPARATION

Mix the butter with the shallots, hazelnuts, and vinegar. Combine with a fork and season well.

OILS & VINEGARS

Keep a selection of oils and vinegars steeped with favorite spices and herbs for marinades and vinaigrettes. Many will keep for up to 1 year in a dark place, though any containing fruits may deteriorate more rapidly. To sterilize containers, boil for 10 minutes, drain, and dry in a low oven.

HERB-INFUSED OIL

This oil will keep for up to 1 month.

INGREDIENTS

a few sprigs of rosemary, thyme, and sage
olive oil

PREPARATION

Place the herbs in a sterilized bottle. Gently heat just enough oil to fill the container until bubbles form around the edge. Bottle, and seal when cool.

ANNATTO OIL

This keeps indefinitely, though the color and aroma fade.

INGREDIENTS

1 cup (250ml) vegetable oil
4 tbsp annatto seeds

PREPARATION

Gently heat the vegetable oil until bubbles form around the edge. Add the seeds and steep for 2–3 hours. Strain into a sterilized bottle, and seal.

OLIVE-OLIVE OIL

This oil will keep for about 2 weeks.

INGREDIENTS

1 cup (125g) black olives in oil
several sprigs of fresh rosemary
olive oil, to cover

PREPARATION

Place the olives and rosemary in a sterilized jar and fill with enough olive oil to cover. Seal and leave for several days to develop the flavors.

SCALLION-STEEPED OIL

An unusual oil that will keep for up to 1 week in the refrigerator, and up to 2 weeks if strained.

INGREDIENTS

1 cup (250ml) vegetable oil
8–10 scallions, thinly sliced

PREPARATION

Gently heat the vegetable oil until tiny bubbles form around the edge. Place the scallions in a bowl and pour over the heated oil. Cool to room temperature and serve with chicken, fish, or Asian dishes.

CLASSIC VINAIGRETTE

This basic recipe can be varied to taste by using any other flavored vinegar. You can also add 2–3 tablespoons of chopped fresh herbs or a finely chopped shallot.

INGREDIENTS

1 tbsp red or white wine vinegar
1 tsp Dijon mustard
1 garlic clove, finely chopped
3 tbsp extra-virgin olive oil
salt and black pepper

PREPARATION

Whisk together the vinegar, mustard, garlic, and oil until the mixture is well blended and the oil has emulsified, then season to taste.

PEAR VINEGAR

INGREDIENTS

1 ripe pear, chopped or thinly sliced
1 tsp sugar
cider vinegar, to cover
¼ cup (60ml) apple or pear juice, optional

PREPARATION

Place the pear and sugar in a large jar. Fill with cider vinegar to cover and add the apple or pear juice, if using. Let steep overnight, then strain, squeezing the solids through cheesecloth. Pour into a sterilized bottle and seal.

VERY BERRY VINEGAR

INGREDIENTS

3–4 tbsp blackberries or raspberries
1 tsp sugar
½ cup (125ml) raspberry or red wine vinegar

PREPARATION

Crush the berries in a bowl and combine with the sugar. Pour over the vinegar and leave overnight. Strain well, pour into a sterilized bottle, and seal.

HOT PEPPER VINEGAR

INGREDIENTS

2–3 tbsp crushed dried chilies
1 bottle of sherry or cider vinegar

PREPARATION

Add the chilies to the vinegar and reseal. It becomes hotter and more flavorful with time.

MIXED HERB VINEGAR

This recipe is a good way to use small quantities of wine left over after a dinner party. The wine enriches the vinegar, giving it a smoother, deeper flavor. The vinegar will keep for 1 month. To keep it longer, strain off the herbs after they have infused the vinegar for a week.

INGREDIENTS

several sprigs of dried or fresh tarragon, rosemary, thyme, basil, or bay leaves
pinch of salt
red or white wine vinegar
red or white wine

PREPARATION

Place the mixed herbs in a sterilized bottle and add the salt. Almost fill the bottle with vinegar, about seven eighths full, then top off with a little wine, using red wine with red wine vinegar, and white wine with white wine vinegar.

Herb-Infused Oil

Mixed Herb Vinegar

Scallion-Steeped Oil

RECIPES

Every country and culture has specialties that are cooked over an open fire. The following recipes are gathered from far-flung cuisines to reflect the diversity and worldwide appeal of barbecue cookery. Though the seasonings vary from delicate to fiery and the techniques from simple to elaborate, the recipes are all enhanced by the aroma of smoke and the distinctive flavors that this method of cooking imparts.

All recipes serve 4 unless otherwise stated.

VEGETABLES

Vegetables taste wonderful cooked on the barbecue, and they need only a short time to marinate. Choose from the best of the season and vary the flavorings to taste: lemon juice, balsamic vinegar, wine, mustard, a few herbs. Cook enough garlic, peppers, and eggplant to last the week and refrigerate – they make wonderful salads and soups.

EGGPLANT & CORN SOUP

This is a bright-tasting hearty soup that is easy to prepare using barbecued vegetables. It is a particularly good soup to make the day after a barbecue, when the vegetables are already cooked.

INGREDIENTS

½ eggplant, cut lengthwise, then scored along the cut side
2 ears of corn
2 tbsp olive oil, plus extra for brushing
salt, to taste
1 onion, chopped
3 garlic cloves, finely chopped
2½ cups (750ml) vegetable or chicken stock
1 large ripe or canned tomato, diced
¼ tsp ground cumin, or to taste
ground cayenne, to taste

PREPARATION

1 Prepare a charcoal fire or preheat a gas grill.
2 Brush the eggplant halves and the shucked corn with olive oil, sprinkle with salt, then cook, preferably covered, over medium-low coals until tender, 10–20 minutes.
3 Remove the vegetables from the barbecue and let cool.
4 When cool, dice the eggplant and scrape the corn from the cobs.
5 Heat the olive oil in a pan and sauté the onion and garlic until softened, then add the stock, tomato, and cumin. Bring to a boil.
6 Reduce the heat and add the eggplant and corn. Continue cooking for another 5–10 minutes to allow the flavors to blend, then season with salt and cayenne to taste. Serve hot.

VARIATION

MEDITERRANEAN FLAVOR Omit the cumin and cayenne. Add 1 zucchini and 1 fennel bulb, grilled and diced, and garnish with shredded basil.

WARM MUSHROOM SALAD WITH PINE NUTS & TARRAGON

This simple-to-prepare dish is full of exciting flavors. Serve it on a bed of crisp greens dressed with nut oil vinaigrette.

INGREDIENTS

6 large stuffing mushrooms
3 cups (150g) mixed curly endive and radicchio, finely sliced
½ bunch (30g) arugula
2 shallots, chopped
1 tbsp hazelnut or walnut oil
3 tbsp pine nuts
Tarragon Marinade
3 garlic cloves, finely chopped
¼ cup (60ml) olive oil
¼ cup (60ml) balsamic vinegar
1 tbsp coarsely chopped fresh tarragon
salt and black pepper

PREPARATION

1 Prepare a charcoal fire or preheat a gas grill.
2 To make the marinade, mix together the garlic, olive oil, half the vinegar, and half the tarragon. Place the mushrooms in a shallow dish, pour over the marinade, and season. Leave for 30 minutes.
3 Drain the mushrooms and cook caps down over medium heat for 4–5 minutes. Turn and cook the other side for the same time.
4 Meanwhile, combine the sliced endive and radicchio with the arugula and shallots. Toss with the remaining balsamic vinegar and the hazelnut or walnut oil.
5 Serve the hot mushrooms with the crisp greens, sprinkled with the pine nuts and the remaining tarragon.

CHARGRILLED RADICCHIO WITH GORGONZOLA

Radicchio, endive, and lettuce or young cabbage are traditionally cooked on the barbecue in the Venezia region of Italy — the bitter flavor mellows as they cook over the fire. Sprinkled with pungent cheese and herbs, they make a wonderful first course.

INGREDIENTS

½ cup (125ml) olive oil
5–8 shallots, chopped
¼ cup (60ml) white wine vinegar
½ tsp herbes de Provence, crumbled
4 heads radicchio, Belgian endive, and young cabbage, halved or quartered
salt and black pepper
¼lb (125g) Gorgonzola or other blue cheese, sliced
fresh basil leaves, to garnish, optional

PREPARATION

1 Prepare a charcoal fire or preheat a gas grill.
2 Mix together the olive oil, shallots, vinegar, and herbs to make a vinaigrette. Brush the radicchio, endive, and cabbage lightly with a little vinaigrette, then cook over medium-high heat until slightly charred, but not overcooked. The heads will become slightly limp as they cook.
3 Remove the vegetables from the barbecue and season. Sprinkle with the remaining vinaigrette and serve with the sliced Gorgonzola and the basil leaves, if using.

VARIATION

NORTH ITALIAN BARBECUE Serve grilled radicchio with Rosemary Polenta (see page 134) and herby sausages (see page 111) for an authentic taste. Substitute a tangy chèvre, such as Montrachet, for the Gorgonzola.

GRILLED ASPARAGUS

For those who have never tried barbecuing asparagus, it is a revelation. The slender stalks remain crisp, and their delicate character is surprisingly enhanced by the heat of the flames.

INGREDIENTS

1–1½lb (500–750g) asparagus, ends trimmed
White Wine Marinade
½ cup (125ml) olive oil
2 tbsp lemon juice or balsamic vinegar
2 tbsp dry white wine
1 tbsp whole-grain or Dijon mustard
2 garlic cloves, finely chopped
large pinch of fresh thyme or marjoram
salt and black pepper

PREPARATION

1 Prepare a charcoal fire or preheat a gas grill.
2 Mix together the marinade ingredients in a shallow dish. Add the asparagus and toss well, then marinate for 10–15 minutes.
3 Drain the asparagus and place on the barbecue when medium-hot. Cook until crisp but cooked through, about 3 minutes on each side, depending on the heat of the flames.

SMOKY-SPICY CORN SALAD

Corn, cooked over charcoal, then brushed with butter and sprinkled with pepper, is a staple street food of Mexico. Here, it is transformed into a zesty salad.

INGREDIENTS

4 ears of corn
1 tbsp butter, softened
2–3 garlic cloves, finely chopped
2–3 scallions, thinly sliced
2 tbsp chopped fresh cilantro
1 tsp ground cumin
⅓ cup (90g) Salsa (see page 124)
juice of ½ lime
⅓ cup (75ml) olive oil
salt and black pepper

PREPARATION

1 Prepare a charcoal fire or preheat a gas grill.
2 Lightly spread the corn with butter, then cook, covered, over medium-hot coals until grill marks form and the corn is tender, 5–8 minutes.
3 Remove from the heat. When cool enough to handle, scrape the corn off the cobs, combine with the remaining ingredients, and season to taste.

BEETS WITH MOROCCAN DRESSING

Beets cooked over the barbecue grow smoky and rich. You can also use canned beets.

INGREDIENTS

4–6 raw, unpeeled beets or peeled, cooked beets
olive oil, for brushing
Moroccan Dressing
3 garlic cloves, finely chopped
1 onion, chopped
1 ripe or canned tomato, chopped
2 tbsp chopped fresh cilantro
¼ tsp ground cumin
¼ tsp curry powder
1 tbsp vinegar or lemon juice
3 tbsp olive oil
pinch of sugar
salt and ground cayenne, to taste

PREPARATION

1 Prepare a charcoal fire or preheat a gas grill.
2 Brush the beets with olive oil and place over medium-low coals. Cook raw beets slowly over low heat until they are easily pierced, 1–1½ hours; precooked beets should be placed over the heat just long enough to develop a smoky aroma, about 5 minutes.
3 Remove from the barbecue, peel if necessary, then cut into thick slices. Blend the dressing ingredients and toss with the beets. Taste for seasoning. Serve warm or at room temperature.

VARIATION

GRILLED POTATOES & PUMPKIN Parboil 4–5 large potatoes, then cut into thick slices. Peel and slice 1 small pumpkin. Marinate in 2 tablespoons of olive oil, 1 tablespoon of lemon juice, and 1 chopped garlic clove. Grill until browned, then toss with the Moroccan Dressing.

GRILLED EGGPLANT SLICES

Barbecued eggplants are highly versatile. Cook them whole or sliced, as here, or purée the smoky flesh to use in dips, sauces, or soups.

INGREDIENTS

1 eggplant, cut crosswise into ½ in (1cm) slices
olive oil, for brushing
2 tbsp red or white wine vinegar, or to taste
½ onion, finely chopped
3–4 tbsp chopped fresh parsley
salt and black pepper
2 garlic cloves, finely chopped, optional

PREPARATION

1 Prepare a charcoal fire or preheat a gas grill.
2 Brush the eggplant slices with olive oil on both sides. Cook over medium-hot coals until the first side has browned and formed grill marks, then turn and cook the other side.
3 Remove from the heat and sprinkle with the vinegar, onion, parsley, salt and pepper, and garlic, if using. Serve at room temperature, either as an appetizer or to accompany roasted meats.

EGGPLANT SALATA

This delectable Middle Eastern dip reminds me of the café in Tel Aviv that I frequented as a teenager.

INGREDIENTS

1 medium-large eggplant, halved lengthwise
olive oil, for brushing
1 garlic clove, finely chopped
3 tbsp tahini
3 tbsp plain yogurt
juice of ½ lemon
½ tsp cumin seeds
salt, to taste
Tabasco or other hot sauce, to taste
lettuce leaves and sprigs of fresh cilantro, to garnish

PREPARATION

1 Prepare a charcoal fire or preheat a gas grill.
2 Score the eggplant flesh deeply without cutting through completely, then brush with olive oil. Cook over medium-hot coals for 10–15 minutes on each side, or until the outside is lightly charred in spots and the flesh is tender. Let cool, then dice.
3 Blend together the garlic, tahini, yogurt, lemon juice, cumin seeds, salt, and Tabasco, and mix with the eggplant. Serve on a bed of lettuce leaves, garnished with cilantro.

CHARGRILLED SCALLIONS

INGREDIENTS

16 scallions, trimmed
Tangy Marinade
2 tbsp Dijon mustard
2 garlic cloves, finely chopped
salt and black pepper
¼ cup (60ml) olive oil
juice of ½ lemon

PREPARATION

1 Prepare a charcoal fire or preheat a gas grill.
2 Combine the marinade ingredients in a shallow dish. Add the scallions and marinate for about 30 minutes.
3 Drain the scallions and cook over hot coals until charred on each side and just tender inside.
4 To serve, cut diagonally into bite-sized lengths.

LEEKS WITH CREAMY BEET VINAIGRETTE

This dish is as beautiful as it is delicious. The vinaigrette can be refrigerated for up to 2 days. The leeks could also be served with Mojo Rojo (see page 125).

INGREDIENTS

8 leeks, trimmed
olive oil, for brushing
salt and black pepper
Beet Vinaigrette
⅓ cup (75ml) light olive oil
5oz (150g) pickled beets, drained and finely chopped
2 shallots, chopped
2 tbsp red or white wine vinegar
pinch of sugar or splash of balsamic vinegar
½ cup (100ml) heavy cream or crème fraîche
3 tbsp chopped chives

PREPARATION

1 Prepare a charcoal fire or preheat a gas grill.
2 Blanch the leeks in boiling water for about 2 minutes, then drain, rinse in cold water, and drain well again. Brush with a little olive oil and sprinkle with salt and pepper.
3 To make the vinaigrette, process the olive oil, beets, shallots, vinegar, and sugar until smooth. Add the cream and process again. Season to taste.
4 Cook the leeks over a hot fire for 2–3 minutes on each side, just long enough to give grill marks and an appealing fire-scented aroma.
5 Serve sprinkled generously with chopped chives, with vinaigrette spooned on each plate.

FIRE-COOKED SHALLOTS

*Shallots cooked on the barbecue are great, their
outer layers slightly charred, their insides
tender and sweet, and they go well with almost
any other dish: steaks, chicken, fish, or an assortment
of vegetables. They also give a smoky, tropical taste
to spicy vegetable soups. Toss an extra handful
of shallots on the fire when barbecuing and
reserve for the next day's stockpot.*

INGREDIENTS

*12–16 large shallots, peeled
3 tbsp olive oil
salt and black pepper*

PREPARATION

1 Prepare a charcoal fire or preheat a gas grill.
Get 4 skewers ready – wooden skewers should be
soaked in cold water for 30 minutes.

2 Blanch the shallots in boiling water for 2–3
minutes, then drain, rinse well in cold water, and
drain again.

3 Thread the shallots on skewers, allowing 3 or 4
per skewer, and brush with olive oil. Cook the
shallots on a medium-cool part of the fire for
10–15 minutes, allowing them to char slightly on
the outside. Covering enhances the smoky flavor
and reduces the cooking time.

4 Remove the shallots from the skewers, sprinkle
with salt and pepper, and serve immediately.

*Fire-Roasted
Cherry
Tomatoes*

*Fire-Cooked
Shallots*

FIRE-ROASTED CHERRY TOMATOES

Skewer the tomatoes to keep them from falling into the fire and for easy removal from the grill.

INGREDIENTS

24–30 cherry tomatoes
salt
2 tbsp olive oil
2–3 garlic cloves, finely chopped

PREPARATION

1 Prepare a charcoal fire or preheat a gas grill. Get 6 skewers ready – wooden skewers should be soaked in cold water for 30 minutes.
2 Thread the tomatoes on the skewers, allowing 4 or 5 tomatoes per skewer.
3 Cook over medium-hot coals, covered if possible, for 5–8 minutes, or until the tomatoes have heated through and split their skins slightly.
4 Serve immediately, sprinkled with salt, olive oil, and garlic, or with a dab of flavored butter (see pages 42–43).

GREEN BEANS WITH GARLIC BUTTER

Green beans are fantastic cooked on the barbecue. Skewer them, or place on a fine wire mesh, to keep them from falling into the fire.

INGREDIENTS

1lb (500g) green beans
4 tbsp butter
4 garlic cloves, chopped or crushed
salt and black pepper

PREPARATION

1 Prepare a charcoal fire or preheat a gas grill. Get 6–8 skewers ready – wooden skewers should be soaked in cold water for 30 minutes.
2 Blanch the beans very quickly in boiling water, just until they turn bright green. Drain, rinse well in cold water, and drain again.
3 Skewer the beans crosswise, threading 5–8 beans on each skewer.
4 Warm the butter in a small pan until melted, then remove from the heat and add the garlic. Brush a small amount of garlic butter on the green beans and keep the remainder warm.
5 Cook the beans quickly over medium-hot coals, 2–3 minutes on each side. Remove the skewers and serve with the remaining garlic butter poured over.

FAR EASTERN BROCCOLI

Broccoli, blanched then quickly barbecued, is a delicious surprise. Cook covered to encourage a smoky flavor.

INGREDIENTS

2lb (1kg) broccoli, divided into florets, stems peeled
Oriental Marinade
1 tbsp sugar
1–2 tsp grated fresh ginger
1 garlic clove, finely chopped
3 tbsp dark soy sauce
2 tbsp sesame oil
1 tbsp balsamic vinegar

PREPARATION

1 Blanch the broccoli quickly in boiling water, just until it turns bright green. Drain immediately and rinse well in cold water or plunge into ice water. Drain well again and place in a shallow dish.
2 Mix the marinade ingredients, pour over the broccoli, and marinate for up to 3 hours.
3 Prepare a charcoal fire or preheat a gas grill.
4 Drain the broccoli and reserve the marinade. Cook the broccoli over high heat for about 1 minute on each side.
5 Arrange the broccoli on serving plates and pour over the reserved marinade.

ROASTED CARROTS

Cooking carrots over the fire concentrates their sweet flavor, and a ginger butter amplifies it.

INGREDIENTS

4 large thick carrots or 8 smaller carrots
salt
3 tbsp butter
1 garlic clove, finely chopped
1 piece preserved ginger, chopped, plus 1 tbsp syrup from the jar

PREPARATION

1 Prepare a charcoal fire or preheat a gas grill.
2 Blanch the carrots in boiling salted water until tender but still crunchy, about 6 minutes. Drain and rinse in cold water. Cut thick carrots in half lengthwise.
3 Heat the butter and garlic for 3 minutes, then add the preserved ginger and the syrup. Remove from the heat and toss the carrots in the mixture.
4 Cook over medium-hot coals, turning once or twice until lightly browned, 6–8 minutes.

STUFFED PEPPERS

*Chilies and peppers roasted on the barbecue develop
a deliciously smoky flavor. The skin separates
from the flesh, especially if cooked under a cover,
making them easy to peel. (This can be done
ahead of time.) Serve with a salad of mixed leaves,
sprinkled with scallions and cilantro,
as a spicy starter, or with Butterflied Leg of Lamb
(see page 96) as a light lunch.*

INGREDIENTS

*8–10 mild chili peppers, such as Anaheim, Poblano,
Thai, or Serrano, or 4 green bell peppers
¼ cup (60ml) olive oil
2 tbsp red or white wine vinegar
3 garlic cloves, finely chopped
1 tbsp fresh oregano, chopped, or
½ tsp dried oregano or marjoram
salt and black pepper
several generous pinches of cayenne
¼lb (125g) mild goat cheese, or more as needed*

PREPARATION

1 Prepare a charcoal fire or preheat a gas grill.
2 Roast the peppers over medium-hot coals,
turning every few minutes until the outside is
evenly charred but the flesh is not burned through,
8–10 minutes. Covering the barbecue will
encourage the skin to separate from the flesh.
3 Place the peppers in a bowl or plastic bag and
seal so that the heat steams off the charred skins.
Let cool for 30–45 minutes. This is best done
ahead of time for maximum flavor and aroma.
4 When cool, peel the peppers, make a lengthwise
slit in the side, and remove and discard the core
and seeds. Arrange in a shallow dish.
5 Blend half the oil and vinegar with the
garlic, oregano or marjoram, salt and pepper, and
cayenne. Pour over the peppers. Leave for 2 hours
at room temperature, or overnight in the
refrigerator.
6 Drain the peppers, reserving the marinade, and
stuff each one with a tablespoon of goat cheese. If
cooking green peppers, stuff each with a quarter
of the cheese, using more to fill them if necessary.
7 Arrange the peppers in a baking dish and pour
over the marinade. Place over medium coals,
covered, or under the broiler for 4–5 minutes, just
long enough to melt the cheese.
8 If making a salad, toss the salad leaves with the
remaining oil and vinegar.
9 Serve the stuffed peppers with a salad of mixed
green leaves, sprinkled with sliced scallions and
chopped cilantro.

Garlic

Red wine
vinegar

Olive oil

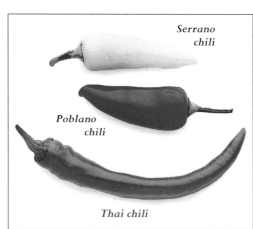

Serrano
chili

Poblano
chili

Thai chili

Oregano

Salt

Black pepper

Cayenne

Goat cheese

ARTICHOKES WITH TOMATO-TAPENADE VINAIGRETTE

This is my own interpretation of a Sicilian peasant dish: the smoke emphasizes the distinctive character of the artichoke. The Tomato-Tapenade Vinaigrette is especially good with artichokes, but mayonnaise, Aïoli (see page 66), or a flavored butter (see pages 42–43) could also be served.

INGREDIENTS

4 artichokes, stems peeled and trimmed and sharp leaf points removed
10 garlic cloves, finely chopped
½ cup (50g) chopped fresh parsley
¾ cup (175ml) olive oil
3 tbsp vinegar
salt and black pepper
Tomato-Tapenade Vinaigrette
1–2 garlic cloves, finely chopped
2 tsp tapenade or other black olive paste
1 tbsp red wine vinegar
1 tbsp tomato purée
1 tbsp chopped fresh parsley
⅓ cup (75ml) olive oil

PREPARATION

1 Prepare a charcoal fire or preheat a gas grill.
2 Cook the artichokes in boiling water for 15 minutes, then drain upside down. Open up the artichoke leaves and pull out the pale inner leaves. Using a teaspoon, scrape out the fuzzy choke (see page 152) and discard. Place in a dish.
3 Mix together the garlic, parsley, oil, vinegar, salt, and pepper. Spoon the mixture into each artichoke, placing some between the leaves. Pour any remaining mixture over the artichokes and leave for a few minutes to marinate.
4 Cook the artichokes over medium-hot coals, turning every so often until they are cooked through and lightly charred in places (the outer leaves will be discarded as you eat the artichokes).
5 To make the vinaigrette, blend the garlic with the tapenade, vinegar, tomato purée, and parsley. Whisk in the oil (it will need to be restirred just before serving).
6 Serve the artichokes with the vinaigrette as a dipping sauce for the leaves.

VARIATION

MEDITERRANEAN ARTICHOKES & SWORDFISH
Instead of the vinaigrette, use the Mediterranean Marinade (see page 59) and add 4 swordfish steaks. Marinate for 3 hours at room temperature, then grill over hot coals for 10 minutes, turning once.

STUFFED EGGPLANT

This dish hails from Sardinia, where eggplants are stuffed with all kinds of savory ingredients, including cheese, salami, ham, and herbs. I have simplified the stuffing to Pesto (see page 124) and cheese. It serves 4 as an appetizer, with roasted peppers, olives, and crusty bread, or 2 as a main course.

INGREDIENTS

3 garlic cloves, finely chopped
6oz (175g) full-flavored cheese, such as fontina or mature Cheddar, grated
3–4 tbsp Pesto (see page 124)
1 medium-large eggplant

PREPARATION

1 Prepare a charcoal fire or preheat a gas grill.
2 Mix together the garlic, cheese, and Pesto.
3 Cut 4 or 5 slashes in the eggplant to form deep pockets. Open up each slash a little with your fingers, then fill with several tablespoons of the cheese mixture.
4 Place the stuffed eggplant in a heatproof baking dish, then spread the remaining cheese mixture over the top. Cook over medium coals, preferably covered, for about 35 minutes, or until the eggplant is cooked through, the cheese has melted, and the cheese topping is crusty.

VARIATION

Leftovers make lovely sandwiches on crusty bread, accompanied by sliced tomatoes, salami, and olives.

NEW POTATOES & YAMS WITH MOJO SAUCES

Mojo sauces are zesty garlicky sauces from the Canary Islands, traditionally eaten with all types of grilled meats, poultry, and fish, as well as with the classic dish of papas arrugadas, or "wrinkled potatoes," so called because cooking the potatoes in salty water makes the skins wrinkle. Here the sauces are paired with a selection of vegetables for a robust starter; add 1–2 lamb chops per person for a full meal.

INGREDIENTS

1lb (500g) new potatoes
2 yams, sliced crosswise and halved
olive oil for brushing
salt for sprinkling
1 yellow pepper, cored, seeded, and cut into strips
To serve
Mojo Rojo and Mojo Verde (see page 125)

PREPARATION

1 Prepare a charcoal fire or preheat a gas grill.
2 Parboil the potatoes and yams until they just begin to give when pierced with a skewer or fork. Drain and let cool for at least 30 minutes.
3 Brush the potatoes and yams with olive oil and sprinkle with salt. Cook over medium-hot coals, turning occasionally, until the vegetables develop grill marks from the barbecue and are cooked through, about 20 minutes.
4 Arrange the vegetables on a platter with one or both of the Mojo sauces and garnish with the strips of yellow pepper.

VARIATION

STEAK WITH CORN & MOJO VERDE Brush 4 steaks and 4 corn cobs with Mojo Verde then with olive oil. Grill over hot coals until the corn is tender and the steaks are browned, but still rare inside, about 4–5 minutes. Serve with Mojo sauce on the side.

MAPLE-ROASTED SWEET POTATOES

The flesh of sweet potatoes varies from almost white to a deep yellowy orange. Choose plump ones with smooth, unwrinkled skins and a strong orange color: the brighter-colored ones have more flavor.

INGREDIENTS

4 sweet potatoes, halved lengthwise
⅓ cup (90g) butter, softened
⅓ cup (90ml) maple syrup

PREPARATION

1 Prepare a charcoal fire or preheat a gas grill.
2 Steam or boil the sweet potatoes until semi-tender, 8–10 minutes, depending on size. Drain and let cool to room temperature.
3 Blend together the butter and maple syrup.
4 Score the cut sides of the potatoes, then spread the butter mixture over all sides.
5 Cook over medium coals, turning once or twice, allowing the outsides to brown and develop grill marks, 6–8 minutes on each side.
6 Remove from the barbecue and serve, spread with the remaining butter and maple syrup.

FIRE-BAKED POTATOES

When I lived on a Greek island, the local café served fire-roasted potatoes as part of its meze. *The proprietor fished a few from the fire, cut them into chunks, sprinkled them with salt, and served them up with a plate of olives and another of greens doused in vinegar. For a richer dish, serve with sour cream seasoned with chopped scallions, chives, and shallots.*

INGREDIENTS

4 medium-large baking potatoes, washed but unpeeled
vegetable oil, for brushing

PREPARATION

1 Prepare a charcoal fire or preheat a gas grill.
2 Prick the potatoes once or twice so they won't burst during cooking, then brush with a little oil.
3 Place the potatoes over medium-low coals and leave, preferably covered, for 40–60 minutes, turning occasionally to make sure that they cook evenly. Alternatively, place in a mound of low coals and leave for 1–2 hours, or until meltingly tender inside. Test with a skewer after 1 hour.
4 Serve hot with either a salad of greens or sour cream flavored with chopped scallions, chives, and shallots.

TWO-BEAN CHEESEBURGERS WITH CHILI AIOLI

These are good the way they are, or serve them sandwiched in a whole-grain bun or crusty roll.

INGREDIENTS

13oz (400g) canned black beans or chickpeas, drained
13oz (400g) canned borlotti or kidney beans, drained
3 garlic cloves, finely chopped
1 onion, grated
1 egg, lightly beaten
1–1½ cups (75–100g) dry bread crumbs
¾ tsp ground cumin
4 tbsp chopped fresh cilantro
salt and ground cayenne, to taste
vegetable oil, for brushing
6oz (175g) mature Cheddar, thinly sliced
To serve
Red Chili Aïoli (see page 124)
lettuce
pickled chilies

PREPARATION

1 Prepare a charcoal fire or preheat a gas grill.
2 Purée the beans in a food processor until they form a chunky paste. Mix in the garlic, onion, egg, bread crumbs, cumin and cilantro, then season with salt and cayenne pepper.
3 Form the mixture into 6–10 patties. Brush with oil and cook over medium-hot coals until lightly browned, 4–5 minutes on each side. When the second side is half browned, about 2 minutes, top each patty with a slice of cheese and continue to cook until the cheese melts.
4 Serve spread with the Aïoli, accompanied by lettuce and pickled chilies.

TOFU TIKKA IN TOMATO-PEA MASALA

Cooking on the barbecue firms up tofu, making it perfect for cutting into smaller pieces and then simmering in a sauce. Here, tikka spices permeate the bland tofu, along with the smoke of the fire. The masala sauce tastes terrific with the smoky spiced tofu.

INGREDIENTS

10oz (300g) firm tofu
Tikka Marinade (see page 35)
Tomato-Pea Masala Sauce
2 tbsp butter
1 onion, chopped
3 garlic cloves, chopped
1 tsp chopped fresh ginger
¼ tsp fennel seeds
¼ tsp garam masala or curry powder
¼ tsp ground coriander
¼ tsp ground cumin
pinch of crushed dried chilies
1 cup (250g) chopped canned tomatoes
¼lb (125g) shelled and blanched fresh peas, or frozen peas
⅔ cup (150g) yogurt
salt
ground cayenne, to taste

PREPARATION

1 Cut the tofu into 4 or 6 large chunks, place in a shallow dish, and rub with the marinade. Let marinate for 1 hour at room temperature, or overnight in the refrigerator.
2 Prepare a charcoal fire or preheat a gas grill.
3 Cook the tofu over medium coals, preferably covered, for 4–5 minutes on each side.
4 Remove the tofu from the barbecue, then let cool. When cool, cut into bite-sized pieces. Barbecued tofu is best the next day, when the flavors have had time to soak in.
5 To make the sauce, melt half the butter in a large skillet and sauté the onion until soft, about 5 minutes. Add the garlic, ginger, and fennel seeds and cook for another minute or two.
6 Stir in the garam masala, coriander, cumin, crushed chilies, and the remaining butter. Cook for a few minutes, then add the tomatoes and peas. Bring to a boil, reduce the heat, and add the tofu pieces.
7 Heat the tofu mixture through, then gently stir in the yogurt, taking care not to break up the tofu. Season with salt and cayenne and serve immediately.

MEDITERRANEAN KEBABS

Any Mediterranean vegetable could be added to these colorful and tasty kebabs.

INGREDIENTS

3–4 zucchini, cut crosswise into ½in (1cm) slices
1 large yellow pepper, cored, seeded, and cut into bite-sized pieces
16 cherry tomatoes
2 onions, cut into chunks
several sprigs of thyme or marjoram
Mediterranean Marinade
5 garlic cloves, finely chopped
3 tbsp balsamic vinegar
⅓ cup (90ml) olive oil
2 tbsp chopped fresh marjoram or thyme
salt and black pepper

PREPARATION

1 Prepare a charcoal fire or preheat a gas grill. Get 8 skewers ready – wooden skewers should be soaked in cold water for 30 minutes.
2 Thread the vegetables onto the skewers with the herb sprigs, alternating the colors, and place in a shallow dish. Combine the marinade ingredients and pour over the skewers. Let marinate for 30 minutes.
3 Drain the kebabs, reserving the marinade, and cook over hot coals for about 5 minutes on each side. Serve hot, with the marinade poured over.

FISH

There are few ways of preparing fish and seafood as appealing or versatile as cooking over hot coals. The method is simple and convenient, needing only an easily prepared marinade and a suitable relish or sauce to serve with the dish – and because you are cooking outside, no fishy smells linger in the kitchen afterward. For best results, oil the grill well, and use a wire grill basket for fragile fillets or whole fish, so that they can be turned easily without disintegrating.

FISH KEBABS

Use fish of differing colors and textures for these kebabs. Shellfish such as shrimp can also be added. The typically Italian inclusion of bread crumbs helps coat the fish and protects it from the hot fire.

INGREDIENTS

6oz (175g) tuna steak, cut into bite-sized pieces
6oz (175g) salmon steaks, skinned, boned, and cut into bite-sized pieces
6oz (175g) cod or other white fish, skinned, boned, and cut into bite-sized pieces
5 garlic cloves, finely chopped
1½ tbsp capers, crushed
juice of ½ lemon
¼ cup (60ml) olive oil
2 tbsp chopped fresh basil, plus several sprigs to garnish
4 tbsp dry bread crumbs
salt and black pepper

PREPARATION

1 Place the tuna, salmon, and cod on a large plate or in a shallow dish.
2 Sprinkle the fish with the garlic, capers, lemon juice, olive oil, chopped basil, the bread crumbs, salt, and pepper. Turn the fish to coat well with the flavorings, then leave for at least an hour to marinate at room temperature, or for up to 12 hours in the refrigerator.
3 Prepare a charcoal fire or preheat a gas grill. Get 8 skewers ready – wooden skewers should be soaked in cold water for 30 minutes.
4 Thread the fish onto the skewers, alternating the different types of fish. Cook over hot coals, preferably covered, until the kebabs are cooked through, 2–3 minutes on each side.
5 Serve the kebabs immediately, garnished with basil sprigs.

MUSTARD-FLAVORED MACKEREL

Mackerel, being strongly flavored and oily in texture, is excellent for barbecuing. Care should be taken, however, as mackerel can fall apart on the grill: oil the surface well before placing the fish on it; alternatively, place the fish on a piece of foil or in a wire grill basket.

INGREDIENTS

2 whole mackerel, cleaned and boned, or 4 mackerel fillets
2 garlic cloves, finely chopped
3–4 tbsp whole-grain mustard
2–3 tbsp olive oil
1–2 tsp sherry vinegar
salt and black pepper
2 tsp chopped chives or fresh parsley

PREPARATION

1 Lay the mackerel flat on a plate.
2 Combine the garlic, mustard, olive oil, and vinegar, then spread over both sides of the fish. Marinate for 30 minutes.
3 Prepare a charcoal fire or preheat a gas grill.
4 Sprinkle the fish with salt and pepper, then cook over hot coals for 4–6 minutes on each side, or until it browns lightly and sizzles.
5 Lift carefully off the barbecue and serve immediately, sprinkled with the chives or parsley.

VARIATION

JAPANESE GRILLED MACKEREL Lay the mackerel fillets in a shallow baking dish. Combine 3 tablespoons each of mirin or medium dry sherry and dark soy sauce with 2 chopped garlic cloves. Bring to a boil, then spoon the hot marinade over the fish and let stand for 30 minutes. Grill the fish over hot coals for 4–6 minutes on each side, until lightly brown and sizzling.

TROUT WRAPPED IN GRAPE LEAVES WITH BEAN SAUCE

*The haunting aroma of grape leaves permeates the flesh
of the trout, giving it a distinctive flavor. Be sure
to peel the fava beans; peeling reveals their lovely green
color and removes the tough outer skin.*

INGREDIENTS

*5 garlic cloves, finely chopped
½ cup (125ml) olive oil
juice of 1½ lemons
4 trout, about 10oz (300g) each, gutted
salt and black pepper
20–24 grape leaves, enough to make 4 bundles; if using
leaves preserved in brine, rinse well, then pat dry
with paper towels
large pinch of sage, fresh chopped, or ½ tsp dried
4 tbsp butter
fresh herb sprigs, to scent the barbecue
3oz (90g) baby fava beans, blanched and peeled
lemon slices and fresh sage sprigs, to garnish*

PREPARATION

1 Mix together half the garlic, 2 tablespoons of oil, and the juice of the half lemon and use to rub the trout inside and out. Season to taste. Stuff each trout with a few rolled-up grape leaves and a little sage, then wrap in grape leaves, leaving the head and tail free (see page 154). If necessary, use string to hold the leaves in place. Let stand for 1–2 hours.
2 To make the sauce, warm the remaining oil, then add the remaining garlic. When fragrant but not brown, remove from the heat and add the butter.
3 Prepare a charcoal fire or preheat a gas grill.
4 Cook the trout over medium-hot coals, adding the herb sprigs to the fire. Turn gently after about 10 minutes. When the leaves are charred around the edges and the fish is firm to the touch, another 5–10 minutes, remove from the heat.
5 Add the beans to the sauce with the juice of 1 lemon. Season and gently warm through.
6 Remove any heavily charred leaves and serve the trout with the bean sauce. Garnish with lemon slices and sage sprigs.

COD WITH SUN-DRIED TOMATO RELISH

Cod is delicious served with this savory paste. When I sampled this dish in the middle of winter — in fact, in the midst of a snowstorm — my first thought was that it tasted of summer.

INGREDIENTS

4 cod fillets, about 1½lb (750g)
salt and black pepper
8–12 basil leaves, shredded
2 tbsp slivered almonds
Sun-Dried Tomato Relish
2 garlic cloves, finely chopped or crushed
10–15 sun-dried tomatoes
1 tbsp capers
3 tbsp olive oil, plus extra for brushing
1–2 tsp sherry or red wine vinegar

PREPARATION

1 Prepare a charcoal fire or preheat a gas grill.
2 To make the relish, purée the garlic using a mortar and pestle or food processor, then add the sun-dried tomatoes, capers, olive oil, and sherry vinegar. Season with pepper and set aside.
3 Brush the cod with a little olive oil, then sprinkle with salt and pepper. Place over hot coals, preferably in a wire grill basket, and cook for 2–3 minutes on each side. Take care that the fish does not overcook, or it will fall apart when you lift it from the barbecue.
4 To serve, spread each fillet lightly with a little Sun-Dried Tomato Relish, then sprinkle with the basil and almonds. Serve immediately.

VARIATION

COD A LA NIÇOISE Omit the flaked almonds and instead serve the cod sprinkled with the basil and surrounded by a handful of young string beans, blanched until tender but still crisp, and mixed salad greens, all tossed in olive oil and vinegar.

CURRIED COD WITH LIME

The longer you let the fish marinate in the spicy mixture, the more flavored it will be. I often prepare this dish the night before and let the cod marinate for 24 hours in the refrigerator. The following evening the fish is ready to be barbecued for a quickly prepared dinner.

INGREDIENTS

½ onion or 5 shallots, finely chopped
2 garlic cloves, finely chopped
½ green chili, such as jalapeño, Kenya, or serrano, chopped, or to taste
2 tsp chopped fresh ginger
1 tsp paprika
1 tsp curry powder or garam masala
½ tsp ground coriander
½ tsp ground cumin
juice of ½ lime
2 tbsp plain yogurt
salt
4 cod fillets, about 1½lb (750g)
Cilantro & Green Chili Butter
(see page 42), cut into thin pats
½ lime, cut into wedges

PREPARATION

1 Purée the onion, garlic, chili, and ginger until it is a fragrant paste, then add the paprika, curry powder, coriander, and cumin and mix in the lime juice. Stir in the yogurt and season with salt.
2 Place the fish fillets in a shallow dish and rub on both sides with the curry mixture until well coated. Marinate at room temperature for 3 hours, or overnight in the refrigerator.
3 Prepare a charcoal fire or preheat a gas grill.
4 Cook the cod over hot coals for 4–6 minutes, preferably covered and in a wire grill basket, turning only once so that fish does not fall apart.
5 Serve hot, with a pat of Cilantro & Green Chili Butter on each fish fillet and a wedge of lime.

CAJUN SPICE FISH & GOLDEN ZUCCHINI

Cajun spices give a delightful zest to cod. Skewers of tiny golden and green squash or slices of pumpkin could be used instead of the zucchini. Serve with a spoonful of Creole Rémoulade (see right) instead of the flavored butter, if you prefer.

INGREDIENTS

4 cod fillets, about 1½lb (750g)
Cajun Spice Rub (see page 40)
2 golden zucchini, sliced into ⅛in (3mm) thick strips
Sun-Dried Tomato & Basil Butter (see page 43)
2 scallions, thinly sliced
1–2 tbsp chopped fresh cilantro

PREPARATION

1 Coat the cod fillets on both sides with three-quarters of the Cajun Spice Rub. Place in a shallow dish and marinate at room temperature for at least 1 hour, or overnight in the refrigerator.
2 Prepare a charcoal fire or preheat a gas grill.
3 Cook the cod fillets over hot coals, preferably in a wire grill basket, for 2–3 minutes on each side until the fish feels firm, turning once.
4 When the fish is half cooked, dust the zucchini with the remaining Cajun Spice Rub and place on the grill. Cook for 2–3 minutes, turning several times, until lightly charred.
5 Serve immediately, with a slice of Sun-Dried Tomato & Basil Butter (see page 43) and a sprinkling of scallions and chopped cilantro.

HADDOCK WITH CREOLE RÉMOULADE

INGREDIENTS

2 tbsp butter
3–4 tbsp black olive paste
2 garlic cloves, finely chopped
1½lb (750g) haddock fillets or steaks
Creole Rémoulade
2 scallions, thinly sliced
4–6 tbsp mayonnaise
1 garlic clove, finely chopped
2–3 tsp wholegrain mustard
1 tsp capers, lightly crushed
½ tsp paprika
black pepper
1–2 tbsp olive oil
juice of ¼ lemon, or to taste

PREPARATION

1 Melt the butter and remove from the heat. Mix with the olive paste and the garlic.
2 Coat the fish fillets with the olive mixture, place in a shallow dish, and leave for at least 30 minutes.
3 Prepare a charcoal fire or preheat a gas grill.
4 To make the rémoulade, mix together the scallions, mayonnaise, garlic, mustard, capers, paprika, and black pepper. Stir in the olive oil until it is absorbed, then add lemon juice to taste.
5 Cook the fish over hot coals, preferably in a wire grill basket, for 2–3 minutes on each side, until lightly browned. Serve the fillets immediately with the rémoulade.

SOLE WITH CAPER & BROWN BUTTER SAUCE

Caper and Brown Butter Sauce is traditionally served with skate, which is not always easy to find. However, the piquant sauce is equally good with the delicate flesh of the sole.

INGREDIENTS

4 fillets of sole, about 1½lb (750g)
salt and black pepper
1 tbsp butter
Caper & Brown Butter Sauce
3 tbsp butter
1–1½ tbsp flavored vinegar, such as raspberry, walnut, or tarragon
1 tbsp capers
2 tbsp chopped fresh parsley

PREPARATION

1 Prepare a charcoal fire or preheat a gas grill.
2 Season the fish and dot with the butter. Set aside while you make the sauce.
3 To make the sauce, melt the butter over medium heat until it turns brown and nutty. Do not let it burn.
4 Add the vinegar to the butter, then remove from the heat. Set aside and keep warm.
5 Place the sole on a well-oiled grill, or preferably in a wire grill basket. Cook, covered if possible, over hot coals until the edges are lightly browned and the fish feels slightly firm to the touch, about 8 minutes. If the fish is cooked covered, there will be no need to turn it.
6 Remove the fish carefully and pour over the sauce. Sprinkle with the capers and parsley and serve immediately.

HERB-CURED BARBECUED SALMON

A light curing with salt and herbs firms and seasons the salmon. The center of the steaks should appear slightly underdone, for maximum flavor and most appealing texture. Serve with a salad of pickled cucumber sprinkled with fresh dill, and black bread with butter.

INGREDIENTS

4 salmon steaks, 6–7oz (175–200g) each
4 tbsp coarse salt
1 tbsp sugar
1 tbsp chopped fresh tarragon
2 tbsp chopped fresh dill or fennel
2 tbsp butter, melted
black pepper, to taste
lemon wedges, to garnish

PREPARATION

1 Place the salmon steaks in a shallow dish and add the salt, sugar, half the tarragon, and half the dill or fennel. Turn to coat well, then marinate at room temperature for 3–5 hours, or overnight in the refrigerator.
2 Prepare a charcoal fire or preheat a gas grill.
3 Brush the salt-sugar-herb mixture off the salmon steaks. Rinse the steaks in cool water, then pat dry with paper towels. Brush them with half the melted butter.
4 Cook the steaks over hot coals for 2–3 minutes until just brown, then turn. Cook on the other side until they feel fairly firm but slightly underdone.
5 Serve the steaks immediately, drizzled with the remaining butter, and sprinkled with black pepper and the remaining tarragon and dill. Garnish with lemon wedges.

SALMON WITH CHERMOULA

Chermoula is a Moroccan seasoning paste used for marinating food, especially fish. I also like using this mixture with whole salmon, tucking it into the cavity to permeate the flesh with its aroma and flavor.

INGREDIENTS

4 salmon steaks, 6–7oz (175–200g) each
Chermoula
4 garlic cloves, finely chopped
½ green chili, such as jalapeño, Kenya, or serrano, finely chopped
3–4 tomatoes, chopped
4 tbsp chopped fresh cilantro
4 tbsp chopped fresh parsley
3 tbsp olive oil
juice of ½ lemon
½ tsp each ground cumin and curry powder
salt, to taste

PREPARATION

1 To make the Chermoula, combine the garlic, chili, tomatoes, cilantro, parsley, 2 tablespoons of olive oil, the lemon juice, cumin, and curry powder. Process until smooth and season to taste.
2 Combine the remaining olive oil with half the Chermoula in a shallow dish. Add the salmon steaks and turn until well coated. Marinate for 1–3 hours at room temperature.
3 Prepare a charcoal fire or preheat a gas grill.
4 Cook the salmon over hot coals, preferably covered, for 8–10 minutes, turning once, until the salmon is opaque and feels fairly firm to the touch.
5 Serve immediately, accompanied by the remaining Chermoula.

SALMON & BACON KEBABS WITH TARRAGON SAUCE

Serve as an appetizer while the rest of the dinner cooks on the barbecue, or as a main course, accompanied by a bowl of Garlic & Scallion Mash (see page 133) and a crisp green salad.

INGREDIENTS

12oz (375g) salmon steaks, cut into about 30 cubes
8 bacon slices
8 cherry tomatoes
2 tbsp olive oil
1 tbsp balsamic vinegar
Tarragon Sauce
3–5 shallots, chopped
1 garlic clove, finely chopped
½ cup (125ml) dry white wine
1 tomato, diced
1 tbsp chopped fresh tarragon, or 3 tbsp dried
1 tbsp chopped fresh parsley
½ cup (125ml) fish stock
salt and black pepper

PREPARATION

1 To make the sauce, combine half the shallots with the garlic, wine, tomato, tarragon, and parsley in a small saucepan. Bring to a boil and cook over high heat for 3–4 minutes until reduced to about 2 tablespoons of liquid.

2 Add the stock and continue to cook over high heat until it reduces again to about 4 tablespoons. Strain and let cool. Season with salt and pepper; it should have a strong, slightly sour, and herby taste.

3 Prepare a charcoal fire or preheat a gas grill. Get 8 skewers ready – wooden skewers should be soaked in cold water for 30 minutes.

4 Thread the skewers, using 1 slice of bacon and 3–4 cubes of salmon per skewer. Alternate the bacon and the salmon, winding the bacon from end to end of each skewer so that it bastes the salmon as it cooks. Place a cherry tomato at the end of each skewer.

5 Lay the skewers on a plate and sprinkle with the remaining shallots, the olive oil and balsamic vinegar, and 3 tablespoons of the Tarragon Sauce. Leave for about 10 minutes, or until ready to cook.

6 Place the skewers over hot coals and cook quickly, turning several times, until the bacon is well browned and the salmon is cooked through, about 6 minutes. Drizzle each skewer with a little of the remaining sauce. Serve immediately with Garlic & Scallion Mash (see page 133) and a crisp green salad.

SALMON BURGERS WITH PESTO & GRILLED ASPARAGUS

These are delightfully elegant burgers compared to the standard hamburger. Asparagus, crisp and hot from the barbecue, and an herby Pesto (see page 124) make this a lovely choice for the first warm evenings of spring.

INGREDIENTS

1lb (500g) salmon fillet or steaks, boned
juice of ½ lemon
1 tbsp butter, softened
1 cup (60g) soft bread crumbs, or more as needed
1 tsp chopped fresh parsley
3 shallots, finely chopped
salt and black pepper
½ bundle asparagus, ends trimmed
1 tbsp olive oil or melted butter
¼ cup (60ml) Pesto (see page 124), or to taste

PREPARATION

1 Chop the salmon into small pieces, then mince in a food processor or by hand.

2 Place the salmon in a bowl and add half the lemon juice. Using a fork, work the butter, bread crumbs, parsley, shallots, salt, and pepper into the salmon, making sure the mixture is thoroughly combined. Form into 4 patties, wrap each in plastic wrap, and then chill in the refrigerator for at least an hour to firm them up.

3 Prepare a charcoal fire or preheat a gas grill.

4 Sprinkle the remaining lemon juice over the asparagus, then drizzle with the olive oil. Sprinkle with salt and pepper. Grill the salmon patties and the asparagus over the hot coals, preferably in a wire grill basket, for about 2 minutes on each side.

5 Serve the patties with a dollop of Pesto on the side, or spread some over each patty.

MONKFISH KEBABS WITH AIOLI

The clean, refreshing quality of tangy Aïoli
makes a delicious foil to rich monkfish.

INGREDIENTS

1½lb (750g) monkfish steaks, cut into chunks
salt, to taste
2 tbsp olive oil
Aïoli
1 garlic clove, crushed
1 large egg
1 tbsp Dijon mustard
juice of ½ lemon
salt and ground cayenne, to taste
¾–1 cup (200–250ml) olive oil

PREPARATION

1 Prepare a charcoal fire or preheat a gas grill. Get 8 skewers ready – wooden skewers should be soaked in cold water for 30 minutes.
2 To make the Aïoli, blend the garlic in a food processor with the egg, mustard, lemon juice, salt, and cayenne.
3 Slowly blend in the oil, a drop or two at a time. Once half the oil has been absorbed, add the rest in a thin stream, allowing it to emulsify before adding more. Blend until thickened, then refrigerate.
4 Thread the monkfish on the skewers. Sprinkle with salt, then brush with olive oil. Cook over hot coals for 3–4 minutes on each side, according to thickness. Serve with the Aïoli, and Mojo Rojo (see page 125) if desired.

SWORDFISH STEAKS FROM THE ISLE OF CAPRI

INGREDIENTS

4 swordfish steaks, about 1½lb (750g)
olive oil, for brushing
Tomato Sauce
13oz (400g) canned chopped tomatoes
3–5 garlic cloves, finely chopped
½ cup (125ml) olive oil
red wine vinegar, to taste
2 tsp anchovy paste, or to taste
black pepper or ground cayenne, to taste
handful of chopped fresh herbs, such as basil,
parsley, marjoram, thyme, mint

PREPARATION

1 Prepare a charcoal fire or preheat a gas grill.
2 To make the sauce, combine the tomatoes, garlic, olive oil, vinegar, anchovy paste, and black pepper or cayenne to taste. Stir in the herbs.
3 Brush the steaks with olive oil, sprinkle with pepper, then cook over hot coals for about 8–10 minutes until just cooked through, turning once.
4 Spoon half the Tomato Sauce over the bottom of a large flat dish.
5 Remove the fish steaks from the barbecue and arrange in the dish in a single layer. Top with the remaining Tomato Sauce.
6 Either serve immediately, or allow the fish steaks to cool to room temperature and absorb the flavors of the sauce, then serve.

WHOLE FISH FROM THE GREEK ISLANDS

These fish are cooked whole on the barbecue, usually basted with olive oil and lemon. For a crisp skin, scrape off the scales with a serrated knife, working from tail to head, then brush the skin with olive oil. Serve with a Greek salad of feta cheese, tomatoes, and olives.

INGREDIENTS

2 whole fish, such as red or gray mullet, red snapper,
or tilapia, about 2lb (1kg) each
juice of 2 lemons
salt and black pepper
½ cup (125ml) olive oil
6 bay leaves, plus extra to garnish
1 tsp dried oregano, crumbled

PREPARATION

1 Prepare a charcoal fire or preheat a gas grill.
2 Score the fish diagonally at 2in (5cm) intervals with a sharp knife. Rub inside and out with half the lemon juice, salt and pepper, and 2 tablespoons of the olive oil. Place the bay leaves inside the fish and sprinkle inside and out with oregano.
3 Place the fish over the hot coals, preferably in a wire grill basket, and cook for 15 minutes on each side for medium-sized fish, or 25 minutes on each side for larger ones.
4 Sprinkle the fish with the remaining olive oil and lemon juice and serve immediately with a Greek salad. Garnish with bay leaves.

PROVENÇAL FISH IN GRAPE LEAVES

Wrapping fish in grape leaves is a favorite method of cooking in Provence. It protects against the heat and allows the fish to absorb the aroma of the smoke and leaves. Serve with salad or a bowl of Aïoli (see page 66).

INGREDIENTS

4 sea bass fillets, about 1½lb (750g)
4 garlic cloves, finely chopped
4 shallots, chopped
2 tbsp olive oil
juice of ½ lemon
2 tsp chopped fresh tarragon, or ½ tsp dried
grated zest of ¼ orange
salt and black pepper
20–24 grape leaves, enough to make 4 bundles; if using
grape leaves preserved in brine, rinse well then
pat dry with paper towels

PREPARATION

1 Place the fish in a shallow dish and sprinkle with the garlic, shallots, olive oil, lemon juice, tarragon, orange zest, and a good sprinkling of salt and pepper. Marinate for 15–30 minutes at room temperature.
2 Prepare a charcoal fire or preheat a gas grill.
3 Place each fish fillet on a grape leaf and wrap up well, using as many leaves as it takes to cover it completely (see page 154). If necessary, use string to hold the leaves in place.
4 Cook the fish bundles over medium-hot coals, preferably covered. It should take 15–20 minutes for the fish to cook through, turning once. Do not allow the fish to overcook.
5 Serve immediately, letting each person unwrap his or her own bundle. Accompany with a salad of orange, tomato, and onion slices, tossed with Classic Vinaigrette (see page 44), or with a bowl of Aïoli (see page 66).

MAYAN SWORDFISH COATED WITH ANNATTO & CHILI

*This traditional recipe, from the Caribbean
shores of Mexico, dates back to Mayan times. It is
one of the most delightfully exotic dishes I know. A
whole fish such as snapper, tilapia, or bass may be used
instead of fish steaks or fillets. Corn tortillas and
black beans make delicious accompaniments.*

INGREDIENTS

*4 tbsp cooked annatto seeds (see page 100),
plus 2 tbsp of the cooking liquid
2 garlic cloves, finely chopped
½ tsp coarse salt
Spicy Mexican Marinade (see page 32)
½ tsp crushed cinnamon
½ tsp ground cloves
4 swordfish steaks, or other fish fillets,
about 1½lb (750g)
handful of bay leaves, to scent the barbecue
bay leaves and lemon wedges, to garnish*
To serve
*1 onion, chopped
1 avocado, diced
2–3 tbsp chopped fresh cilantro
2 ripe tomatoes, diced
pickled chilies, diced*

PREPARATION

1 Purée the annatto seeds and the liquid with the
garlic and salt, then mix with the Spicy Mexican
Marinade, adding the cinnamon and cloves.
2 Rub the annatto-spice mixture on both sides of
the fish steaks. Place in a shallow dish and marinate
at room temperature for 30–60 minutes, or in the
refrigerator for up to 3 hours.
3 Prepare a charcoal fire or preheat a gas grill.
4 If using dried bay leaves, soak them in cold
water until softened. Place the bay leaves on the
coals to produce fragrant smoke.
5 Remove the fish steaks from the marinade.
Cook the steaks over medium-hot coals for about
5 minutes, until golden brown and cooked through
on one side, then turn, using a large spatula, and
cook the other side.
6 Serve immediately, sprinkled with chopped
onion, avocado, cilantro, tomatoes, and pickled
chilies. Garnish with bay leaves and lemon wedges.

VARIATION

MAYAN FISH WITH TROPICAL FLAVORS To serve,
omit the diced vegetables. Drizzle unsweetened
canned coconut milk over the hot fish and serve
with diced banana and tomato and lime wedges.

Garlic

Annatto liquid

Annatto seeds

Swordfish steaks

Spicy Mexican
Marinade

Cinnamon

Ground cloves

Bay leaves

Coarse salt

SCALLOPS WITH GINGER-COCONUT SAUCE

INGREDIENTS

1lb (500g) scallops
2 scallions, thinly sliced
2 tbsp coarsely chopped peanuts
1 tbsp chopped fresh mint
Ginger-Coconut Sauce
½ cup (125ml) sweet white wine, such as muscatel
½ cup (125ml) fish or chicken stock
2 tsp chopped fresh ginger
5 shallots, chopped, or 1 onion, chopped
1 cup (250ml) unsweetened coconut milk
large pinch of saffron, soaked in
2 tbsp hot water, or a pinch of turmeric
grated zest of ¼ lime
juice of ½ lime, or to taste

PREPARATION

1 To make the sauce, combine the wine, stock, ginger, shallots, and coconut milk in a small saucepan and bring to a boil. Cook over high heat until the onion is cooked through and the sauce has thickened, about 6 minutes.
2 Add the saffron liquid and the lime zest to the sauce, and heat through, then season with the lime juice to taste. Strain the mixture if you prefer a smooth sauce.
3 Prepare a charcoal fire or preheat a gas grill. Get 8 skewers ready – wooden skewers should be soaked in cold water for 30 minutes.
4 Thread the scallops on the skewers and cook over medium-hot coals, 2–3 minutes on each side for small scallops, 4–5 minutes for larger ones, until slightly firm and lightly charred. Serve immediately with the sauce and sprinkled with the scallions, peanuts, and mint.

SCALLOPS WITH WILD MUSHROOM SAUCE

Mushrooms and cream are luxurious partners for the even more luxurious scallop. I find that the sweet cream and the woody flavor of mushrooms enhance the sweetness of the scallop. Cook the scallops and the mushrooms on skewers so that they do not fall into the fire.

INGREDIENTS

2 tbsp butter
1 garlic clove, finely chopped
½ tsp chopped fresh rosemary
2 tsp chopped fresh parsley
juice of ¼ lemon
salt and black pepper
1lb (500g) scallops
¼lb (125g) mushrooms
Wild Mushroom Sauce (see page 126)

PREPARATION

1 Prepare a charcoal fire or preheat a gas grill. Get 8 skewers ready – wooden skewers should be soaked in water for 30 minutes.
2 Melt the butter in a small saucepan, but do not let it brown. Swirl the garlic, rosemary, and parsley into the hot butter, then season with lemon juice, salt, and pepper.
3 Brush the scallops with the flavored butter.
4 Thread the mushrooms and scallops on the skewers. Cook over medium-hot coals, 2–3 minutes on each side for small scallops, 4–5 minutes for larger ones.
5 Meanwhile, heat the Wild Mushroom Sauce.
6 When the scallops are slightly firm and lightly charred and the mushrooms cooked through, serve immediately with the sauce.

MUSSEL BROCHETTES FROM THE COTE D'AZUR

Barbecuing mussels on the open fire is one of the most delicious ways to cook them. In this dish the light marinade of fennel-scented fresh tomato sauce adds moisture, while the bacon bastes the mussels with its savory juices.

INGREDIENTS

2lb (1kg) mussels, scrubbed and debearded
2 garlic cloves, finely chopped
½ tsp fennel seeds, crushed or ground
¼ tsp herbes de Provence, or to taste
12oz (375g) canned chopped tomatoes
3 tbsp olive oil
1 tbsp mild vinegar, or to taste
4–6 tbsp toasted bread crumbs
8 slices of bacon

PREPARATION

1 Prepare a charcoal fire or preheat a gas grill. Get 8 skewers ready – wooden skewers should be soaked in cold water for 30 minutes.
2 Place the mussels over medium-low coals for 8–10 minutes, preferably covered, until they open. Shell them, discarding any that fail to open.
3 Purée the garlic with the fennel seeds. Add the herbs, tomatoes, olive oil, and vinegar and purée again until fairly smooth. Spoon half the mixture over the mussels in a shallow dish and marinate at room temperature for 30 minutes.
4 Remove the mussels from the sauce and dredge in bread crumbs.
5 Using 1 slice of bacon per skewer, alternate bacon and mussels, winding the bacon from one end of each skewer to the other, with bread-crumbed mussels in between.
6 Cook over hot coals, preferably covered, for 5–6 minutes or until the bacon is browned and the mussels are crispy. Serve immediately with the remaining sauce.

SARDINIAN LOBSTER WITH OLIVE OIL, LEMON, & TOASTED CRUMBS

I enjoyed this wonderful dish on a beach in Sardinia. The lobster was bathed in olive oil, lemon, and herbs, then sprinkled with crumbs and roasted over the fire.

INGREDIENTS

1 garlic clove, finely chopped
¾ cup (175ml) olive oil
juice of 2 lemons, or to taste
½–1 tsp herbes de Provence
salt and black pepper
2 lobsters, prepared and split (see page 154)
4–6 tbsp dry bread crumbs
lettuce leaves and lemon slices, to garnish

PREPARATION

1 Prepare a charcoal fire or preheat a gas grill.
2 Combine the garlic with the olive oil, lemon juice, and herbes de Provence and season to taste.
3 Gently loosen the meat in the lobster shells with a paring knife. Stir the olive oil mixture well, then drizzle about half over the lobster meat.
4 Pat the bread crumbs over the lobsters and cook over medium-hot coals, covered, until the bread crumbs are lightly browned and crisp.
5 Serve immediately, garnished with lettuce leaves and lemon slices, with the remaining olive oil mixture as a sauce for spooning over as desired.

VARIATION

THAI LOBSTER For a completely different flavor, omit the garlic, olive oil, lemon, and herb dressing, and the bread crumbs. Instead, combine the Thai Marinade (see page 16) with ½–¾ cup (125–175ml) canned, unsweetened coconut milk. Spoon half this mixture evenly over the lobster halves, then cook as above over medium-hot coals until the tops are lightly browned. Serve the remaining Thai mixture as a sauce with the cooked lobster.

Whole Fish from the Greek Islands (see page 67)

Mussel Brochettes from the Côte d'Azur (see page 71)

Sardinian Lobster with
Olive Oil, Lemon, &
Toasted Crumbs
(see page 71)

MALAYSIAN CHILI SHRIMP

A spicy marinade enhances the sweet flavor of shrimp. Serve as an appetizer with lettuce and a sprinkling of scallions, or with rice as a main course.

INGREDIENTS

2 tbsp chopped fresh ginger
4 garlic cloves, finely chopped
2 tbsp vegetable oil
¼–⅓ cup (75–90ml) ketchup
3 tbsp vinegar (preferably fruit or mild)
3 tbsp soy sauce
3 tbsp sugar
1 tsp crushed dried red chilies, or to taste
½ tsp ground cayenne, or to taste
¼–½ tsp Szechuan peppercorns, lightly toasted and crushed
½ tsp five-spice powder
2 tsp sesame oil
1½lb (750g) raw jumbo shrimp, peeled but with tails left on

PREPARATION

1 Mix together the ginger, garlic, oil, ketchup, vinegar, soy sauce, sugar, crushed chilies, cayenne, Szechuan peppercorns, five-spice powder, and sesame oil.
2 Place half the mixture with the shrimp in a shallow dish and toss until well coated. Let marinate for 30–60 minutes at room temperature.
3 Prepare a charcoal fire or preheat a gas grill. Get 8 skewers ready – wooden skewers should be soaked in cold water for 30 minutes.
4 Thread the shrimp on skewers and cook over hot coals, turning them once or twice, for 2–3 minutes on each side, or until they become opaque and pink.
5 Brush the hot shrimp with the remaining marinade, and serve on a bed of lettuce, sprinkled with scallions.

CHILI-CITRUS SHRIMP SKEWERS WITH BACON & MANGO SALAD

These spicy skewers make an excellent appetizer.

INGREDIENTS

1lb (500g) raw peeled jumbo shrimp
Spicy Mexican Marinade (see page 32)
½lb (250g) bacon
2 heads curly endive, lightly dressed in oil and lime juice
2 mangoes, sliced
scallions and fresh cilantro, chopped, to garnish

PREPARATION

1 Toss the shrimp in the marinade in a shallow dish, then let marinate for 30–60 minutes at room temperature.
2 Prepare a charcoal fire or preheat a gas grill. Get 8 skewers ready – wooden skewers should be soaked in cold water for 30 minutes.
3 Thread the shrimp on each skewer with a slice of bacon, alternating the bacon with the shrimp and winding the bacon from one end of the skewer to the other.
4 Cook over hot coals for 3–5 minutes, until the bacon is browned and the shrimp are just opaque.
5 Serve immediately, on a bed of curly endive tossed with sliced mango. Garnish with chopped scallions and cilantro leaves.

OYSTERS WITH SPINACH RELISH

While fresh oysters are almost unbeatable, the scent of smoke enhances their flavor in this extravagant dish.

INGREDIENTS

48 oysters in their shells
Spinach Relish
½ garlic clove, finely chopped
large pinch of fennel seeds
3 tbsp cooked, chopped, squeezed-dry spinach
1 tbsp chopped fresh tarragon
3 tbsp butter, melted
juice of ¼ lemon, or to taste
salt and black pepper

PREPARATION

1 Prepare a charcoal fire or preheat a gas grill.
2 Purée the garlic with the fennel seeds, spinach, and tarragon, then mix well with the melted butter. Add lemon juice, salt, and pepper to taste.
3 Place the oysters on the grill over medium coals until they open, 8–10 minutes. Carefully remove from the heat and serve with the Spinach Relish.

CHILI-CITRUS SQUID

For ease of preparation, buy the squid already cleaned. Alternatively, see page 154 for instructions on how to prepare squid. Leave the squid bodies whole and include the tentacles.

INGREDIENTS

3 garlic cloves, finely chopped
3 kiwi fruit, peeled and mashed
2 clementines, peeled, diced, and mashed
juice of ½ lime
large pinch of cumin seeds
½–1 green chili, such as Thai or Scotch bonnet, finely chopped
3 tbsp olive oil, plus extra for drizzling
salt, to taste
1lb (500g) small squid, cleaned (see page 154)
paprika, to taste
chopped fresh cilantro, scallions and
wedges of lime, to garnish

PREPARATION

1 Purée the garlic, then place in a shallow dish with the kiwi fruit, clementines, lime juice, cumin seeds, chili, olive oil, and salt.
2 Add the squid, turn to coat, and marinate for 30–60 minutes. Do not marinate longer or the squid will lose its firm texture.
3 Prepare a charcoal fire or preheat a gas grill.
4 Cook the squid over hot coals for 2–3 minutes on each side, until just opaque and lightly marked from the grill. Take care that the tentacles do not fall through the holes of the grill.
5 Serve immediately, sprinkled with paprika and drizzled with olive oil. Garnish with cilantro, scallions, and lime wedges.

VARIATION

SQUID SALAD This makes an ideal hot-weather salad. Serve the squid on a bed of curly endive tossed with Classic Vinaigrette (see page 44). Accompany with crusty bread.

LOBSTER WITH ROASTED GARLIC & CILANTRO BUTTER

Garlicky butter sauce is good with whole lobsters and lobster tails; the latter are sold frozen raw, so that when you barbecue them they cook rather than just warm through, as whole lobsters do when they have been parboiled. Serve the smoky-flavored lobster with hot and spicy Chipotle Salsa (see page 77) and warm corn tortillas (easily heated on the barbecue) for lobster tacos.

INGREDIENTS

12 garlic cloves, roasted until lightly
charred and soft
4 garlic cloves, finely chopped
6 tbsp chopped fresh cilantro
½ green chili, finely chopped, or to taste
juice of ½ lemon
1 cup (250g) butter
salt, to taste
2 large lobsters, halved lengthwise (see page 154)
or 4 medium–large lobster tails

PREPARATION

1 Prepare a charcoal fire or preheat a gas grill.
2 Squeeze the soft garlic from the roasted cloves (see page 152), then purée with the chopped garlic, cilantro, green chili, and lemon juice.
3 Melt the butter but do not let it brown. Add to the garlic mixture and mix well until smooth. Add salt to taste.
4 Spoon about half the butter sauce onto the cut lobster halves or tails, making sure that the fragrant mixture gets into all the crevices.
5 Place the lobster over the hot coals, preferably covered, for 10–15 minutes until heated through and lightly golden in places. If using lobster tails, cook for 15–20 minutes until they turn bright red. If cooking uncovered, turn once to mark the top of the lobster lightly with grill marks. Keep the butter sauce warm on top of the barbecue.
6 Serve immediately, with the butter sauce for dipping, Chipotle Salsa (see page 77), and warm corn tortillas.

VARIATION

MONKFISH WITH ROASTED GARLIC & CILANTRO BUTTER Spread 2lb (1kg) monkfish tails with a little of the butter. Place the fish, rounded side up, on a grill over hot coals for a few minutes to sear, then turn. Spread the cooked side generously with the butter and cook for about 7 minutes, or until the fish is just cooked through and the topping has a light crust.

SEAFOOD WITH MANGO-PEPPER RELISH

INGREDIENTS

5 tbsp butter

3 garlic cloves, finely chopped

1 tbsp thinly sliced fresh ginger

24 mussels, cooked and shelled (see page 71)

4 scallops

12 raw jumbo shrimp in their shells

1 crab, shell and claws cracked

4 squid, cleaned (see page 154) and cut into pieces

thin strips of lemon and lime zest, to garnish

Mango-Pepper Relish

large pinch of salt

1 small onion, chopped

½ green chili, such as Thai or serrano, chopped

½ red pepper, roasted, peeled, seeded, and finely chopped

1 tbsp olive oil

1 large ripe, firm mango, peeled, pitted, and diced

juice of 1 lime, or to taste

2 tbsp shredded fresh mint

PREPARATION

1 Prepare a charcoal fire or preheat a gas grill.

2 To make the relish, purée 2 garlic cloves with the salt, then add the onion and green chili and purée again until it forms a paste.

3 Add the red pepper, olive oil, and mango, then season to taste with lime juice. Sprinkle with mint and set aside.

4 Melt the butter in a small saucepan until it foams, but do not allow it to brown. Remove from the heat and stir in the remaining garlic and ginger. Set aside and keep warm.

5 Skewer the mussels, scallops, and shrimp or place in a wire grill basket so that they do not fall into the fire, then place with the crab and squid over medium-hot coals, preferably covered so that the smoke can flavor the flesh. Cook for 4–5 minutes on each side.

6 Serve immediately with the ginger-garlic butter and the Mango-Pepper Relish. Garnish with thin strips of lemon and lime zest.

SPICY SEAFOOD SOUP WITH GREEN BEANS

The basis of this soup is a Mexican technique for creating complex flavors: heat a small amount of oil in a pan, then ladle in several spoonfuls of spicy salsa. The heat of the oil "fries" the sauce, reducing it to a concentrated paste. When stock is added it produces a soup with a rich, full-bodied flavor.

INGREDIENTS

1 squid, cleaned (see page 154), including tentacles
¼lb (125g) scallops, halved if very large
10 raw jumbo shrimp in their shells
1lb (500g) mussels, scrubbed and debearded
10 clams or crab claws, well scrubbed
2 tbsp vegetable oil or olive oil
4–6 tbsp Chipotle Salsa (see right)
1 quart (1 liter) fish stock
1 small onion, peeled and
sliced crosswise
½ tsp cumin seeds, or to taste
salt, to taste
2oz (60g) green beans, preferably haricots
verts, frozen or fresh
1 tbsp chopped fresh cilantro
4 lime wedges, to garnish

PREPARATION

1 Prepare a charcoal fire or preheat a gas grill.
2 Skewer the squid, scallops, and shrimp or place in small wire grill baskets so that they do not fall into the fire. Cook the shellfish over medium-hot coals, preferably covered to give a smokier flavor, beginning with the mussels (cook about 10 minutes in total) and clams or crab claws (10 minutes), then adding the shrimp (about 5 minutes), and finally the squid and scallops (about 3 minutes). Remove from the heat when the mussels and clams have opened and the shrimp have turned pink. Discard any shellfish that fail to open.
3 Heat the oil in a large pan and, when smoking, add the salsa. Cook the salsa in the oil, letting it reduce in volume and concentrate in flavor. When it is little more than a thick paste, add the stock, onion, cumin seed, and salt. Bring to a boil, cook for 5 minutes to allow the flavors to blend, then add the green beans.
4 Meanwhile, cut the squid into rings or bite-sized pieces, then add it to the soup along with the rest of the cooked shellfish and heat through. The green beans should be just tender but still almost crisp and bright green in color.
5 Serve immediately in bowls, sprinkled with cilantro and garnished with wedges of lime.

GRILLED MUSSELS WITH CHIPOTLE SALSA

This makes a sumptuous appetizer; for a main dish, double the amount and serve a flavorful rice or pasta alongside.

INGREDIENTS

1lb (500g) mussels, scrubbed and debearded
salt
Chipotle Salsa
4–5 ripe tomatoes, diced
1–2 dried chipotle chilies, cut into small pieces
½ cup (125ml) water
3 garlic cloves, finely chopped
salt, to taste
½ onion, finely chopped

PREPARATION

1 Prepare a charcoal fire or preheat a gas grill.
2 Meanwhile, make the Chipotle Salsa. Place the tomatoes, chipotle chilies, and water in a small pan. Bring to a boil and cook over high heat until the tomatoes are just cooked through and the chilies are softened, 5–7 minutes. Remove from the heat.
3 Purée the garlic with a generous sprinkling of salt, then add the onion and purée again. A mortar and pestle is best for this process as it draws out the fragrant oils much more efficiently, but a food processor will also do.
4 Strain the tomato-chili mixture, reserving the liquid, and add to the raw onion-garlic mixture. Purée, then stir in the reserved liquid. Add salt to taste and set aside.
5 Place the mussels over medium-low coals and cook, preferably covered, until they open, 8–10 minutes. Discard any that fail to open.
6 Serve the mussels in their shells, with the Chipotle Salsa for dipping.

POULTRY

Chicken, turkey, and duck are most enticing cooked on the barbecue. Crisp-skinned and succulent, they slowly turn a rich brown hue. The variety of flavors is enormous, from strongly spiced chili mixtures to delicate buttery sauces. Poultry should never be overcooked, as it then becomes dry and tasteless. Test with a skewer, removing from the heat as soon as the juices run clear.

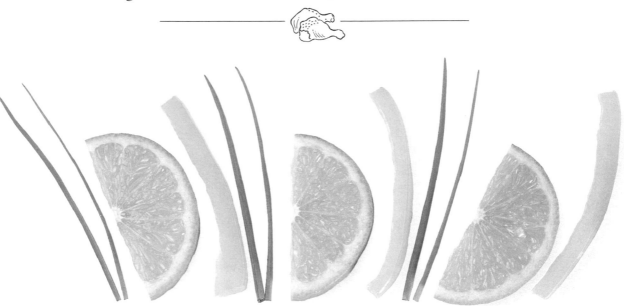

CHICKEN WITH GARLIC, LIME, & TARRAGON

Make this a whole meal by cooking small leeks and peppers alongside the chicken on the barbecue – I especially like a combination of yellow and green peppers, for color as well as flavor. For a richer flavor, add a nugget of Tarragon Butter (see page 42) to melt onto the hot chicken.

INGREDIENTS

4 chicken quarters, about 10oz (300g) each
8–10 garlic cloves, finely chopped
4 lime quarters
salt and black pepper
¼ cup (60ml) dry white wine
⅓ cup (90ml) olive oil
1 tbsp chopped fresh tarragon
8 small leeks, trimmed
1 yellow pepper, cored, seeded, and cut into bite-sized chunks
1 green pepper, cored, seeded, and cut into bite-sized chunks
Tarragon Butter (see page 42), optional
1 tbsp chopped chives

PREPARATION

1 Prepare a charcoal fire or preheat a gas grill.
2 Place the chicken in a shallow dish and sprinkle with the garlic. Squeeze the lime quarters over the chicken, then cut into small pieces and add to the dish, along with the salt, pepper, wine, olive oil, and half the tarragon. Let marinate for 2 hours or more. If marinating overnight, add only half the lime zest, as its oils can be quite strong.
3 Blanch the leeks for 1 minute in boiling salted water, then drain, rinse in cold water, and drain again.
4 Remove the chicken from the marinade and pat dry. Brush the leeks and peppers with the marinade.
5 Place the chicken over hot coals to sear the skin, then move to medium heat and grill slowly, turning occasionally, preferably covered, until cooked through and the juices run clear when pierced with a skewer, 15–25 minutes.
6 Add the leeks 10 minutes before serving, then a few minutes later add the peppers. Cook until the vegetables are slightly browned and just tender. Serve the chicken with a nugget of Tarragon Butter, if desired, and sprinkle with the remaining tarragon and the chives.

BASQUE CHICKEN

Roasted, marinated peppers, combined with Pesto, make a zesty, easily prepared sauce for barbecued chicken.

INGREDIENTS

4 chicken quarters, about 10oz (300g) each
5 garlic cloves, finely chopped
2 tbsp white wine
salt and black pepper
¼ cup (60ml) Pesto (see page 124)
¼ cup (60ml) olive oil
1 green pepper, roasted, peeled, cored, seeded,
and cut into thin strips
1 red pepper, roasted, peeled, cored, seeded,
and cut into thin strips
2 tbsp wine vinegar or balsamic vinegar

PREPARATION

1 Place the chicken in a shallow dish. Blend together 2 of the garlic cloves, the white wine, salt and pepper, half the Pesto, and half the olive oil. Pour this marinade over the chicken, turn to coat, and leave for at least 30 minutes at room temperature, or overnight in the refrigerator.
2 Combine the peppers with the vinegar and half the remaining garlic. Season to taste and let marinate for at least 30 minutes, or overnight.
3 Prepare a charcoal fire or preheat a gas grill.
4 Combine the remaining Pesto with the remaining garlic and olive oil and set aside.
5 Cook the chicken over medium-hot coals, beginning with legs and thighs. Cook for 10 minutes, turning occasionally, then add breast portions and continue until it is all cooked through and the juices run clear when pierced with a skewer, another 10–15 minutes.
6 Combine the peppers with the Pesto mixture and serve spooned over the hot chicken.

CHICKEN WITH WATERCRESS SAUCE

Chicken tastes marvelous with this watercress sauce. Cook the sauce briefly, to preserve its delicate freshness.

INGREDIENTS

4 chicken quarters, about 10oz (300g) each
3 garlic cloves, finely chopped
juice of ¼ lemon
2 tbsp olive oil
Watercress Sauce
4 tbsp butter
2 shallots, chopped
1 garlic clove, finely chopped
1 bunch watercress, washed, dried, and coarsely chopped
1½ cups (400g) crème fraîche or light sour cream
salt and black pepper
juice of ½ lemon, or to taste

PREPARATION

1 To make the sauce, melt the butter over low heat, add the shallots and garlic, and cook gently until softened but not brown. Add the watercress, stir for 1–2 minutes, then remove from the heat.
2 Stir in the crème fraîche, mix well, then season and add lemon juice. Blend in a food processor until smooth, then set aside to cool.
3 Place the chicken in a shallow dish, sprinkle with the garlic, lemon juice, and olive oil and season to taste. Marinate for at least an hour, or in the refrigerator for up to 2 days.
4 Prepare a charcoal fire or preheat a gas grill.
5 Cook legs and thighs over medium coals for 10 minutes, preferably covered, turning occasionally. Add the breasts and cook for another 10–15 minutes or until the juices run clear when pierced with a skewer. Warm the sauce and serve poured over the chicken.

CHICKEN WITH MUSTARD & GARLIC

INGREDIENTS

4 chicken quarters, about 10oz (300g) each
8 garlic cloves, thinly sliced
3 shallots, finely chopped
2–3 tbsp paprika
5 tbsp tarragon mustard or other mild mustard
3 tbsp strong Dijon mustard
3 tbsp olive oil
2 tbsp lemon juice
3 tbsp crème fraîche or light sour cream
salt and black pepper

PREPARATION

1 Place the chicken in a shallow dish. Mix the garlic, shallots, paprika, half the tarragon mustard, the Dijon mustard, oil, and lemon juice in a bowl, add to the chicken and turn to coat. Cover and leave overnight in the refrigerator.
2 Prepare a charcoal fire or preheat a gas grill.
3 Grill legs and thighs over medium-hot coals for 10 minutes, turning once, then add the breasts and grill for 10–15 minutes, or until the juices run clear.
4 Mix the reserved mustard with the crème fraîche, spread over the hot chicken, and season well. Serve immediately.

CHICKEN BREASTS STUFFED WITH MUSHROOMS

This dish was inspired by a damp autumn forage for wild mushrooms. When the stuffed breasts are cooked quickly on the barbecue, the chicken is permeated with the fragrance of the mushrooms.

INGREDIENTS

6–8 dried or fresh morel mushrooms
6–8 cèpes (porcini) or 6 slices dried cèpes
4 boned chicken breasts, skinned
1 shallot, chopped
2 garlic cloves, finely chopped
2 tbsp olive oil
juice of ¼ lemon
salt and black pepper
Shallot Butter (see page 42), with 1 tbsp chopped red chili added to the mixture
lettuce leaves and chives, to garnish

PREPARATION

1 If using dried mushrooms, pour boiling water over them, cover, and let soften for 30 minutes. Drain and squeeze out the excess liquid. Coarsely chop the mushrooms and set aside.
2 Prepare a charcoal fire or preheat a gas grill.
3 Cut a pocket lengthwise in each chicken breast, then fill each pocket with a quarter of the mushrooms (see opposite). Secure with toothpicks, then arrange the breasts in a shallow dish.
4 Mix together the shallot, garlic, olive oil, lemon juice, salt, and pepper. Pour over the chicken breasts and turn to coat well. Marinate at room temperature for at least 1 hour.
5 Cook the chicken breasts over hot coals for about 4 minutes on each side, until they are just cooked through and the juices run clear when pierced with a skewer. Do not overcook.
6 Serve with slices of the Shallot Butter and garnish with lettuce leaves and chives.

CHICKEN BREASTS WITH PESTO

These tender morsels evoke the flavors of the Mediterranean. Serve with fresh pasta tossed with cream, Roquefort, and pine nuts.

INGREDIENTS

4 boned chicken breasts, with skin
2 tbsp white wine
2 tbsp olive oil
salt and black pepper
2 garlic cloves, finely chopped
2–3 tbsp Pesto (see page 124)

PREPARATION

1 Place the chicken breasts in a shallow dish and add the wine, olive oil, salt, and pepper. Turn to coat, then marinate for at least 1 hour.
2 Prepare a charcoal fire or preheat a gas grill.
3 Gently loosen the skin of each chicken breast down one side to make a pocket. Mix the garlic and Pesto and stuff a quarter into each pocket.
4 Cook over medium-hot coals until the chicken is just opaque, the skin is lightly marked from the grill, and the juices run when the flesh is pierced with a skewer, about 8 minutes. Serve immediately.

VARIATION

CHICKEN BREASTS WITH RED PESTO Combine 3–4 chopped sun-dried tomatoes, 1 chopped tomato, and 2 tbsp Pesto. Stuff the chicken breasts as above.

CHICKEN WITH CHIVES & TARRAGON

The marinade gives a delightful yet unobtrusive sweetness to this chicken dish. I prefer to leave the skin on as it helps to hold in the juices of the meat during cooking.

INGREDIENTS

4 boned chicken breasts, with skin
Chive & Tarragon Marinade
3 tbsp sweet white wine, such as Beaumes de Venise
3 tbsp olive oil
2 tbsp chopped chives
1 tbsp chopped fresh tarragon, or ½ tsp dried
grated zest of ¼ orange
salt and black pepper

PREPARATION

1 Arrange the chicken breasts in a shallow dish. Mix together the marinade ingredients and pour over the chicken. Turn to coat, then marinate at room temperature for 1–3 hours, or overnight in the refrigerator.
2 Prepare a charcoal fire or preheat a gas grill.
3 Cook the chicken breasts quickly over hot coals, turning once or twice, until the juices run clear when the flesh is pierced with a skewer. The white flesh should be just turning opaque, the skin striped with marks from the grill, about 8 minutes. Do not allow them to overcook.
4 Serve immediately, with rice and a green salad.

STUFFING CHICKEN BREASTS

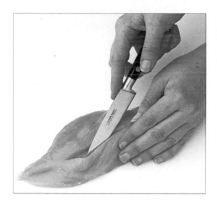

1 Using a sharp knife, cut a lengthwise slit in each chicken breast to form a pocket for the stuffing.

2 Carefully open out each pocket with the knife and fill with a quarter of the chopped mushrooms.

3 Secure the opening with a few toothpicks, to keep the stuffing in place while cooking.

Chicken Breasts Stuffed with Mushrooms

PAILLARDS OF CHICKEN WITH RASPBERRY-GARLIC BUTTER

A piece of meat pounded very thin is called a paillard. Paillards can be duck, beef, veal, lamb, or turkey, but these days are most often chicken. Because paillards are very thin they cook extremely quickly on the barbecue. The result is moist and tender.

INGREDIENTS

2 chicken breasts, boned, skinned, and halved
⅓ cup (90ml) olive oil
3 garlic cloves, finely chopped
2 tbsp raspberry vinegar
4–6 fresh tarragon sprigs
salt and black pepper
Raspberry & Roasted Garlic Butter (see page 43)
handful of roasted garlic cloves (see page 152)
and fresh raspberries, to garnish

PREPARATION

1 Prepare a charcoal fire or preheat a gas grill.
2 Place the chicken breasts between 2 sheets of waxed paper or plastic wrap and gently pound flat with a rolling pin. Place in a shallow dish with the olive oil, garlic, raspberry vinegar, half the fresh tarragon, and salt and pepper to taste. Turn the paillards to coat well, then marinate for 30 minutes–1½ hours.
3 Remove the paillards from the marinade and grill very quickly over hot coals, about 2 minutes on each side.
4 Place the paillards on individual plates and top with a slice of Raspberry & Roasted Garlic Butter to melt in. Garnish with a few roasted garlic cloves and raspberries, and the remaining tarragon.

VARIATION

HERBED CHICKEN PAILLARD WITH CILANTRO & GREEN CHILI BUTTER Use white wine instead of vinegar in the marinade and add 3 tablespoons chopped cilantro, 2 tablespoons chopped basil, and 1 tablespoon chopped sage, marjoram, or thyme. Serve the chicken with slices of Cilantro & Green Chili Butter (see page 42).

DOWN-HOME TEXAS BBQ CHICKEN

Barbecued chicken is a great favorite in Texas, where whole chickens are roasted over a fire to a crisp-skinned bronze. A spicy dry rub is the secret to the Texan flavor, and this one (on quarters for easier cooking) comes from Galveston. The barbecue sauce is not added before cooking: the long grilling would burn the sugar. Instead, brush some on during the last 5 minutes.

INGREDIENTS

4 chicken quarters, about 10oz (300g) each
She-Devil Barbecue Sauce (see page 127)
Galveston Dry Rub
1 tbsp salt
1 tbsp paprika
1 tbsp sugar
1 tbsp mustard powder
1½ tsp grated lemon zest
½ tsp ground cayenne
½ tsp white pepper
½ tsp black pepper
1 tsp crumbled dried bay leaf
6 garlic cloves, finely chopped

PREPARATION

1 Mix together the dry rub ingredients. Rub the mixture over the chicken pieces and let stand for at least 1 hour, or overnight in the refrigerator.
2 Prepare a charcoal fire or preheat a gas grill.
3 Cook the legs and thighs over medium-hot coals for 10 minutes, turning occasionally. Add the breasts and cook for another 15 minutes, or until bronzed but not charred. Test with a skewer: the juices should run clear.
4 About 5 minutes before the end, brush with the barbecue sauce and cook until the chicken chars lightly. Serve with the remaining sauce.

VARIATION

BBQ BRISKET Cook a large brisket in stock until tender, then drain and marinate overnight in the barbecue sauce. Cook slowly over medium-low coals and serve sliced, coated with the sauce.

CARIBBEAN SPICY CHICKEN WINGS

Barbecuing is one of the best ways of preparing chicken wings. They turn out succulent yet crisp and make an excellent appetizer. Wings are also delicious with Szechuan Marinade (see page 86) or Teriyaki Marinade (see page 35).

INGREDIENTS

2lb (1kg) chicken wings, wing tips removed and wings divided at the joint
Cajun Spice Rub (see page 40)
Caribbean Marinade
juice of 2–3 lemons
1 onion, grated
6 garlic cloves, finely chopped
½ tsp ground cumin
1 tbsp syrup from a jar of preserved ginger
¼ tsp cinnamon
¼ tsp ground cayenne
1 tbsp vegetable oil

PREPARATION

1 Mix together the marinade ingredients in a large bowl. Add the chicken wings, toss to coat well, then marinate for 1–3 hours at room temperature, or in the refrigerator overnight.
2 Prepare a charcoal fire or preheat a gas grill.
3 Remove the chicken wings from the marinade and dust with the Cajun Spice Rub.
4 Cook over a hot fire, turning once or twice until the wings are crisp and browned, about 15 minutes. Serve immediately.

AZERBAIJANI-STYLE KEBABS

Traditionally, these fragrant kebabs are served with mild onion slices, wedges of lemon or lime, a plate of fresh herbs such as tarragon, watercress, cilantro, mint, and chervil, and either soft or crisp flat bread.

INGREDIENTS

4 boned, skinned chicken breasts or 1lb (500g) white turkey meat, cut into bite-sized pieces
3 tbsp butter, melted
Azerbaijani Marinade
¾ cup (175g) plain yogurt
½ onion, finely chopped
5 garlic cloves, finely chopped
2 tsp paprika
¼–⅓ tsp saffron, soaked in 1 tbsp warm water
5–6 tbsp chopped fresh mint
1 tsp salt
several dashes of Tabasco or other hot sauce

PREPARATION

1 Mix together the marinade ingredients.
2 Place the chicken in a shallow dish, add the marinade, and toss well. Marinate at room temperature for at least 3 hours, or in the refrigerator overnight or up to 2 days.
3 Prepare a charcoal fire or preheat a gas grill. Get 8 skewers ready – wooden skewers should be soaked in cold water for 30 minutes.
4 Thread the chicken pieces on the skewers, then place over a plate for a few minutes to allow the excess marinade to drip off.
5 Brush the kebabs with the melted butter and cook over hot coals, turning once or twice until the kebabs are lightly browned, about 5 minutes on each side, depending on the heat of the fire.

SKEWERS OF CHICKEN LIVERS, SAUSAGE, & BACON

This makes an enticing party dish, served with a thick slice of Italian or French bread.

INGREDIENTS

1 garlic clove, finely chopped
2 tbsp mild Dijon mustard
1 tbsp chopped fresh rosemary
1 tsp chopped fresh parsley
6 tbsp unsalted butter, softened
salt and black pepper
8 bacon slices
4 Toulouse or Italian fennel sausages, cut into 1in (2.5cm) chunks
10oz (300g) chicken livers, cut into bite-sized pieces

PREPARATION

1 Prepare a charcoal fire or preheat a gas grill. Get 8 skewers ready – wooden skewers should be soaked in cold water for 30 minutes.
2 Mix the garlic, mustard, rosemary, and parsley with the softened butter, blending it well. Season and set aside.
3 Thread the bacon, sausage, and chicken livers onto the skewers, allowing half a sausage and 1 slice of bacon per skewer. Weave the bacon in and out of the sausage and livers, so that it bastes the livers while cooking.
4 Cook over hot coals, turning several times so that they cook evenly, about 5 minutes on each side, or until the bacon is crisply browned, the sausage cooked through, and the livers still pink inside. During the last 2–3 minutes, slather a little of the butter on top of the kebabs. Serve hot, with the remaining butter spread on top to melt in.

GRILLED GAME HENS WITH PROVENÇAL HERBS

Restaurants in the hillside villages of Provence specialize in dishes cooked over an open fire of scented wood, then seasoned generously with local herbs.

INGREDIENTS

4 tbsp unsalted butter
1½ tbsp flavored wine vinegar, such as rosemary or garlic (see pages 44–45)
4 garlic cloves, finely chopped
4 Cornish game hens, split and flattened (see page 155)
salt and black pepper
2 tsp mixed dried herbs, including thyme, marjoram, rosemary, fennel, and savory
½ tsp dried crumbled bay leaves
fresh basil leaves
fresh rosemary sprigs, to garnish

PREPARATION

1 Prepare a charcoal fire or preheat a gas grill.
2 Gently heat half the butter in a small saucepan, then add the vinegar and garlic. Cook for 1–2 minutes, then remove from the heat.
3 Sprinkle the hens with salt and pepper, rubbing it in well, then brush all over with the flavored butter and sprinkle with dried herbs.
4 Loosen the skin in places along the breast and thighs, making small pockets. Stuff a small knob of the remaining butter and a few basil leaves into each pocket. With a sharp knife, make small slits over the rest of the hen and insert butter and basil as before. Marinate at room temperature for 30–60 minutes.
5 Barbecue over medium-hot coals for 20–30 minutes until golden brown on the outside, but still juicy inside, turning occasionally. The hens are cooked if the juices run clear when the thigh is pierced with a skewer. Serve garnished with rosemary sprigs.

VARIATION

MOROCCAN-FLAVOR GAME HENS Soften 4 tbsp butter, then blend into it 8 finely chopped garlic cloves, 2 tbsp chopped cilantro, 6 finely chopped scallions, 1 tbsp paprika, 1 tsp ground cumin, salt and ground cayenne to taste, and the juice of 1 lime. Rub this flavored butter all over the split and flattened hens, then marinate for at least 3–4 hours in the refrigerator. Grill over medium-hot coals for 20–30 minutes, turning several times, until the juices run clear when the thigh is pierced with a skewer. Serve with Tomato & Ginger Chutney (see page 128).

Garlic

Wine vinegar

Butter

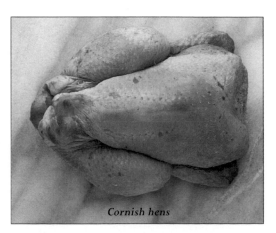

Cornish hens

Dried herbs

Bay leaves

Basil

Rosemary sprigs

Black
pepper

Salt

INDONESIAN GAME HENS

Throughout Indonesia, chicken, game hens, quail, and birds of all kinds are marinated in spicy-sweet mixtures, then barbecued. You can smell them cooking over braziers set out on street stands, where their aroma beckons irresistibly. Serve with steamed rice, bean sprouts, and a crisp salad.

INGREDIENTS

4 Cornish game hens, split and flattened (see page 155)
Indonesian Marinade (see page 36)

PREPARATION

1 Place the split hens in a large shallow dish. Pour on the marinade and turn to coat well. Marinate for at least 3 hours at room temperature or overnight in the refrigerator.
2 Prepare a charcoal fire or preheat a gas grill.
3 Cook over hot coals, turning once or twice, until just cooked through, 10–15 minutes on each side. Serve with steamed rice, crisp bean sprouts, and Cucumber, Carrot, Red Cabbage, & Green Mango Salad (see page 134).

CHICKEN TIKKA

This kebab is traditionally prepared in a kilnlike tandoori oven. A covered barbecue works equally well, sealing in the juices and adding a smoky scent. Serve with Middle Eastern Spiced Pilaf (see page 133) and Cucumber-Yogurt Relish (see page 129).

INGREDIENTS

4 boned, skinned chicken breasts, about 2lb (1kg), cut into bite-sized pieces
juice of 1 lemon
2 tbsp melted butter
Tikka Marinade
⅔ cup (150g) plain yogurt
3 garlic cloves, finely chopped
2 tsp ground coriander
½ tsp turmeric
1½ tsp ground cumin
1½ tbsp paprika
¼ tsp ground ginger
large pinch of ground cayenne
1 tbsp tamarind paste or mango chutney
To serve
salt
fresh mint leaves, chopped
fresh cilantro leaves, chopped
½ cucumber, diced
lemon wedges

PREPARATION

1 Place the chicken in a shallow dish; pour over the lemon juice, and let stand for 15–30 minutes.
2 Mix the marinade ingredients, pour over the chicken, and turn to coat well. Marinate for 3 hours, or overnight in the refrigerator.
3 Prepare a charcoal fire or preheat a gas grill. Get 8 skewers ready – wooden skewers should be soaked in cold water for 30 minutes.
4 Thread the chicken pieces on the skewers. Pat with paper towels to remove the surface marinade, then brush with melted butter.
5 Cook over hot coals, preferably covered, turning several times, until the kebabs are just done, about 3 minutes on each side. Serve sprinkled with salt, chopped mint and cilantro leaves and cucumber. Garnish with lemon wedges.

SZECHUAN CHICKEN & SHIITAKE MUSHROOMS

Serve with Chinese "crispy seaweed" – finely shredded green cabbage, deep-fried and drained on paper towels.

INGREDIENTS

4 chicken legs and 4 thighs, boned and cubed
4 scallions, cut into 3in (7cm) lengths
½lb (250g) shiitake mushrooms
Szechuan Marinade
1 tsp Szechuan peppercorns, dry-toasted and ground
⅓ cup (90ml) vegetable oil
3 tbsp rice wine or sherry
⅓ cup (90ml) soy sauce
6 garlic cloves, finely chopped
1½ tsp five-spice powder
1 tbsp chopped fresh ginger
3 tbsp sugar
several dashes of Tabasco or other hot sauce
grated zest of ½ orange

PREPARATION

1 Mix the marinade ingredients together.
2 Place the chicken, scallions, and mushrooms in a shallow dish, add the marinade, and coat well. Marinate for 3 hours or up to 24 hours in the refrigerator, turning occasionally.
3 Prepare a charcoal fire or preheat a gas grill. Get 8 skewers ready – wooden skewers should be soaked in cold water for 30 minutes.
4 Thread the chicken, scallions, and mushrooms on the skewers. Cook over medium-hot coals for about 3 minutes on each side, until the chicken is browned and cooked. Serve with "crispy seaweed" scattered with toasted almonds.

CHICKEN WINGS SATAY

INGREDIENTS

2lb (1kg) chicken wings, divided at the large joint
6 garlic cloves, finely chopped
2 tbsp chopped fresh ginger
⅓–½ cup (90–125g) sugar, or to taste
¼ cup (60ml) dry sherry or rice wine
½ cup (125ml) dark soy sauce
2 tbsp sesame oil
6 scallions
Indonesian Peanut Sauce (see page 124)

PREPARATION

1 Place the chicken, garlic, ginger, sugar, sherry, soy sauce, and sesame oil in a shallow dish. Toss well, then marinate for at least 3 hours.
2 Prepare a charcoal fire or preheat a gas grill.
3 Grill the chicken over hot coals for about 10 minutes, or until browned and crisp, turning occasionally. Add the scallions near the end of the cooking time. Serve with the sauce.

TURKEY BURGERS

INGREDIENTS

1lb (500g) ground turkey
1 onion, finely chopped
She-Devil Barbecue Sauce (see page 127)
½ tsp ground cumin, or to taste
1 tbsp vegetable oil
salt and ground cayenne, to taste

PREPARATION

1 Prepare a charcoal fire or preheat a gas grill.
2 Mix the turkey with the onion, 3 tablespoons of sauce, and the cumin. Shape into 4 patties.
3 Brush the patties with oil, then cook over hot coals for 3 minutes on each side. To serve, sprinkle with salt and cayenne and brush with the remaining barbecue sauce.

BANGKOK-STYLE TURKEY WITH THAI DIPPING SAUCE

This spicy coconut marinade is also good with chicken, quail, and the other poultry that appears skewered and barbecued on Bangkok's enticing food stands. Steamed basmati rice and a green salad make the perfect accompaniments.

INGREDIENTS

1 turkey thigh, about 2lb (1kg), boned (see page 155)
and sliced into thin strips
1 zucchini, sliced lengthwise
1 red pepper, cored, seeded, and cut into strips
1 green pepper, cored, seeded, and cut into strips
Thai Dipping Sauce (see page 126), to serve
Bangkok Marinade
2 shallots, finely chopped
4 tbsp chopped fresh cilantro
1½–2 tbsp chopped fresh ginger or galangal
4 garlic cloves, finely chopped
1 tsp diced lemon zest
juice of 1 lemon
3–4 tbsp soy sauce
1 cup (300ml) canned, unsweetened
coconut milk
4 tbsp sugar
1 red chili, chopped, or to taste

PREPARATION

1 Mix together the marinade ingredients in a shallow dish. Add the turkey strips and toss well. Let marinate for at least 3 hours at room temperature or overnight in the refrigerator.
2 Prepare a charcoal fire or preheat a gas grill.
3 Just before cooking, toss the zucchini and peppers in a little of the marinade.
4 Cook the turkey and vegetables over medium-hot coals, turning once or twice, until the vegetables become charred and tender and the turkey is cooked through, 15–20 minutes. Serve with the Thai Dipping Sauce.

Indonesian Peanut Sauce
(see page 124)

Szechuan Chicken & Shiitake
Mushrooms (see page 86)

Chicken Wings Satay
(see page 87)

Bangkok-Style Turkey
with Thai Dipping
Sauce (see page 87)

TURKEY STEAKS WITH HUMMUS

This recipe is inspired by Middle Eastern dishes such as Circassian chicken. It is a tangy, refreshing dish, full of lightness and flavor. Serve with Rosemary Focaccia (see page 118) and a salad of ripe tomatoes.

INGREDIENTS

1 lb (500g) turkey breast, cut into 4 steaks, about
¼–½ in (5mm–1cm) thick
2 garlic cloves, finely chopped
½ cup (125g) hummus
2 tbsp olive oil
juice of ½ lemon
salt
Tabasco or other hot sauce
handful of arugula leaves
2 tbsp chopped fresh cilantro
black olives, to garnish

PREPARATION

1 Prepare a charcoal fire or preheat a gas grill.
2 Place the turkey steaks in a shallow dish with the garlic and half the hummus. Turn to coat, then marinate for 30–60 minutes.
3 Wipe the steaks dry with paper towels, then brush with olive oil. Cook quickly over medium-hot coals for about 3 minutes on each side, until the turkey is cooked through but still juicy.
4 Remove from the heat, then sprinkle the turkey with lemon juice and season with salt and Tabasco to taste. Spread with the remaining hummus, top with arugula and cilantro, and garnish with olives.

THANKSGIVING TURKEY

This serves 12–14. Accompany with Maple-Roasted Sweet Potatoes (see page 58), Baked Potatoes (see page 58), Fire-Roasted Cherry Tomatoes (see page 53), and a relish (see pages 128–29).

INGREDIENTS

½ cup (125g) butter, softened
1–2 tbsp chopped fresh sage
1 turkey, about 12–14lb (5.5–6.5kg)
salt and black pepper
1 onion, cut into chunks
2 celery ribs, cut into chunks
3 garlic bulbs
2–3 rosemary sprigs
½ bottle white wine, approximately

PREPARATION

1 Blend the butter with the sage, then spread over the turkey, inside and out, and season. Place the onion, celery, garlic, and rosemary inside the turkey and pour in ½ cup (125ml) white wine. Secure the opening with a skewer.
2 Place a drip pan under the turkey (see page 147) and half-fill with wine. Cook, covered, over indirect heat, allowing 12 minutes per 1lb (500g), until the turkey is golden brown and cooked through. Test with a skewer in the thickest part of the thigh; the juices should run clear.
3 Let the turkey stand for 10 minutes, then carve. Skim the fat from the drip pan juices, boil to reduce slightly, and pour over.

CHILI-CHEESE STUFFED TURKEY BREASTS

These stuffed breasts are delicious and surprisingly simple to prepare. Serve with warm corn tortillas sprinkled with sliced scallions and topped with sour cream. For a spicier dish, serve with a selection of salsas (see pages 124–25) and Tabasco.

INGREDIENTS

1 lb (500g) turkey breast, sliced into 4 steaks
3 garlic cloves, finely chopped
1 fresh chili, chopped
salt
3 tbsp chopped fresh cilantro
⅓ cup (150g) mozzarella or fontina, cut into 4 slices
1–2 tsp cumin seed
1 tbsp olive oil
2 ripe tomatoes, diced

PREPARATION

1 Prepare a charcoal fire or preheat a gas grill.
2 Place the turkey breasts between waxed paper or plastic wrap, or inside a plastic bag. With a rolling pin or butcher's mallet, lightly pound the turkey to about half its thickness.
3 Sprinkle each turkey slice with garlic, chili, salt, and half the cilantro, then cover one half of the turkey with a cheese slice, leaving a border around the edge. Fold over the turkey and press the edges together.
4 Sprinkle the top of the bundles with cumin seed and drizzle olive oil over. Cook over medium-hot coals, turning after about 4 minutes to cook the other side. The cheese should be melted and the turkey just cooked through.
5 Serve immediately, sprinkled with the remaining cilantro, diced tomatoes, and salt to taste.

YUCATECAN TURKEY

The sweet, garlicky, fruit and spice marinade
originated on the Caribbean shores of Mexico. The turkey
emerges from the barbecue richly flavored,
meaty rather than poultrylike.

INGREDIENTS

1 turkey thigh, about 2lb (1kg), boned (see page 155),
and sliced into steaks ¼ in (5mm) thick

Yucatecan Marinade
12 garlic cloves
½ cup (125ml) pineapple juice
2 tbsp dark brown sugar
juice of ½ lemon or lime
juice of ½ orange
½ tsp each ground cinnamon, ground cloves,
and dried thyme
¼ tsp Tabasco or other hot sauce
½ tsp salt
¾ tsp black pepper

PREPARATION

1 To make the marinade, roast 10 garlic cloves, unpeeled, in a dry pan for about 10 minutes until they are slightly charred and softened. Allow the garlic to cool, then squeeze out the flesh from the skins and mash (see page 152). Chop the remaining garlic cloves.

2 Arrange the turkey steaks in a large shallow dish. Mix the roasted garlic flesh and the chopped garlic with the other marinade ingredients. Pour the marinade over the turkey, turn to coat well, and let marinate at room temperature for 2 hours.

3 Prepare a charcoal fire or preheat a gas grill.

4 Remove the turkey from the marinade and pat dry with paper towels. Cook over hot coals, beginning with the skin side down. Move the steaks around on the grill, turning frequently so that they cook evenly, 15–20 minutes.

5 Serve the turkey steaks hot, with a spoonful of Pickled Onion Rings (see page 129) and another of Guava-Apple Relish (see page 128).

DUCK WITH LAVENDER, THYME, HONEY, & LEMON

A classic Provençal dish. Serve with Fire-Baked Potatoes (see page 58) and roasted peaches.

INGREDIENTS

1 duck (giblets included), about 4lb (2kg), halved
2 onions, chopped
1 bouillon cube
1 quart (1 liter) water
1 tbsp butter
3 tbsp brandy
Provençal Marinade
salt and black pepper
6 garlic cloves, finely chopped
3 shallots, chopped
1 tsp dried lavender, crushed
1 tsp thyme
½ tsp dried herbes de Provence, or 2 tbsp mixed fresh herbs
2 tbsp honey
1½ lemons, halved

PREPARATION

1 To marinate the duck, sprinkle with salt and pepper, half the garlic, the shallots, half the lavender, the thyme, dried herbs, and half the honey. Squeeze the juice of 1 lemon over the duck and add the lemon shells, cut into small pieces. Marinate for at least 3 hours, or overnight in the refrigerator.
2 Meanwhile, place the duck giblets, half the onion, the bouillon cube, and the water in a pan. Bring to a boil, skim, then simmer for 1 hour.
3 Prepare a charcoal fire or preheat a gas grill.
4 Remove the duck from the marinade and dry on paper towels. Place a drip pan under the grill and fill with about 3in (7cm) water or stock. Cook over medium coals, covered if possible, for about 30 minutes, or until the duck is lightly browned and glazed and the juices run clear if the flesh is pierced with a skewer. Cut into portions and keep warm. Skim the fat off the drip pan liquid.
5 To make the sauce, sauté the remaining onion in butter until soft, then add the reserved garlic, lavender, and honey. Add the brandy, simmer for a few minutes, then strain the hot stock and add a ladleful. Boil to reduce, then add another ladleful.
6 Stir in the drip pan liquid. Continue to add stock and reduce it 2–3 more times until the sauce is concentrated in color and flavor. Strain, return to the pan and warm through. Add a squeeze of lemon juice to the sauce, then pour over the duck and serve immediately, with Fire-Baked Potatoes (see page 58) and roasted peaches.

MANGO-MUSTARD GLAZED DUCK

The spicy-sweet hot glaze adds just the right accent to this succulent dish. For a lean meat alternative try rabbit: cook for the same length of time, brushing with the glaze after the first 20 minutes.

INGREDIENTS

1 duck, about 4lb (2kg), cut into halves or quarters
2 tbsp salt
1 tbsp sugar
black pepper
Mango-Mustard Glaze (see page 41)

PREPARATION

1 Place the duck in a shallow dish and sprinkle with the salt, sugar, and black pepper. Marinate at room temperature for at least 3 hours, or overnight in the refrigerator.
2 Prepare a charcoal fire or preheat a gas grill.
3 Rinse the duck well, then dry on paper towels. Place over medium-hot coals and cook slowly, turning and moving the pieces frequently so that the fat does not flare up and burn the flesh. Cook the duck for about 20 minutes, or until the skin is lightly golden.
4 Brush the glaze over the duck and continue cooking for another 15–20 minutes, or until glazed but not burned. Serve immediately.

POMEGRANATE-CRANBERRY DUCK WITH SWEET BASIL

Duck is delectable marinated in tangy-sweet pomegranate syrup (grenadine) and wine, then grilled and served with a cranberry sauce. The sprigs of fresh basil, added at the last moment, perfume the dish with their sweet flavor and aroma. Serve the duck with Garlic & Scallion Mash (see page 133).

INGREDIENTS

1 duck, about 4lb (2kg), cut up and breasts cut in half
Pomegranate & Wine Marinade (see page 37)
handful of basil sprigs, to serve
Sauce
½ cup (125ml) chicken or duck stock
½ cup (125ml) red wine
1 cup (125g) cranberries
1 tbsp sugar
2 shallots, chopped
salt and black pepper

PREPARATION

1 Place the duck pieces in a shallow dish and pour over the marinade. Turn until the duck is well coated, then cover and leave in the refrigerator for at least 12 hours.

2 Prepare a charcoal fire or preheat a gas grill.

3 Remove the duck pieces from the marinade and dry on paper towels. Cook slowly over medium coals, covered and over a drip pan if possible, for about 30 minutes, turning so that the fat is rendered out and the skin browns. Test the legs and thighs with a skewer: the juices should run clear.

4 Slice the breasts very thin and keep the duck warm while you make the sauce.

5 Skim the fat off the drip pan liquid, if using. Combine the liquid with the stock, wine, ¾ cup (90g) of the cranberries, the sugar, and shallots and bring to a boil. Cook the sauce over high heat until it has reduced by half. Taste for seasoning.

6 Serve the duck with the sauce and the sprigs of basil. Garnish with the remaining cranberries.

MEAT

All meat seems to be at its best cooked on the barbecue: crusty on the outside, juicy and succulent within, scented with the smoke of the fire. Marinades and sauces – from simple wine marinades to pungent Central American jerks and elaborate spicy concoctions from the Middle East – enhance the possibilities.

BARBECUED HOISIN LAMB

Hoisin is one of the classic barbecue sauces of China. Sweet, tangy, and spicy hot, it is made from finely ground soy beans. For a vegetarian dish, serve the tofu on its own, surrounded by the grilled mushrooms, onions, and eggplants. Accompany with bean sprouts and steamed rice.

INGREDIENTS

8–12 fresh or dried shiitake mushrooms, stems removed
1½lb (750g) lamb chops or cutlets
9½oz (285g) tofu, cut into thick slices or fingers
about 5 x 3in (12 x 7cm)
Hoisin Marinade (see page 35)
1 tbsp soy sauce
1 tbsp sesame oil
2 onions, halved
4 small Asian or Japanese eggplants, sliced through
but left attached at the stem, then pressed open
to form fans
fresh cilantro leaves, to garnish

PREPARATION

1 If using dried mushrooms, soak in warm water for 30 minutes, then drain and squeeze dry.
2 Place the lamb and tofu in a shallow dish, add half the marinade, and turn to coat well. Leave for at least 4 hours at room temperature or in the refrigerator overnight.
3 Prepare a charcoal fire or preheat a gas grill.
4 Blend together the soy sauce and sesame oil. Brush the mushrooms, onions, and eggplants with this mixture.
5 Cook the lamb, tofu, and vegetables over hot coals. Each item should take 3–4 minutes on either side. As the various ingredients become tender and brown, move to a cooler part of the grill until they are all done.
6 When the chops are almost ready, brush with the remaining hoisin mixture. Serve the chops, tofu, and vegetables with bean sprouts and steamed rice and garnish with fresh cilantro leaves.

PROVENÇAL LAMB

These tender lamb chops exude the flavor of the Mediterranean. I like to eat them with my fingers.

INGREDIENTS

1½–2lb (750g–1kg) lamb chops or cutlets
3½oz (100g) green olive paste (tapenade)
1½ tbsp herbes de Provence
2 tbsp olive oil
2 tbsp balsamic vinegar
5 garlic cloves, finely chopped
black pepper, to taste
½ cup (15g) fresh basil leaves, thinly sliced or torn

PREPARATION

1 Place the lamb in a shallow dish with the olive paste, herbes de Provence, olive oil, vinegar, garlic, and black pepper and mix well. Let marinate for at least 2 hours.
2 Prepare a charcoal fire or preheat a gas grill.
3 Grill the chops over hot coals for 3–4 minutes on each side, depending on their thickness, so the meat is still rare. Serve sprinkled with basil.

LAMB CHOPS WITH GREEN MASALA

Serve these curry-scented little chops with Roasted Carrots (see page 53) and new potatoes.

INGREDIENTS

2lb (1kg) lamb chops or cutlets
Green Masala Marinade (see page 34)

PREPARATION

1 Place the lamb in a shallow dish with the marinade and turn to coat well. Marinate for at least 3 hours, or overnight in the refrigerator.
2 Prepare a charcoal fire or preheat a gas grill.
3 Cook over hot coals for 3–4 minutes on each side, until crusty brown. Serve immediately.

BARBECUED LAMB NOISETTES

A red wine marinade enhances the flavor of lamb.

INGREDIENTS

4 medium or 8 small lamb noisettes
5 shallots, finely chopped
1 garlic clove, finely chopped
⅓ cup (90ml) red wine
1–2 tsp dried tarragon or thyme
2 tbsp olive oil
salt and black pepper
mâche, to garnish

Pink Peppercorn Butter Sauce
2 shallots, finely chopped
1 garlic clove, finely chopped
1½ tbsp pink peppercorns
1½ tbsp chopped fresh parsley
¾ cup (175g) butter, softened
lemon juice, to taste

PREPARATION

1 Place the lamb in a shallow dish with the shallots, garlic, red wine, and tarragon. Turn to coat well, then let marinate at room temperature for 30–60 minutes, or overnight in the refrigerator.

2 To make the butter sauce, mash the shallots, garlic, peppercorns, and parsley into the softened butter and mix well. Add lemon juice to taste, to give a soft texture.

3 Prepare a charcoal fire or preheat a gas grill.

4 Remove the lamb from the marinade and rub well with olive oil.

5 Cook the noisettes quickly over hot coals for about 4–5 minutes on each side, until the meat is just cooked through, dark and crusty on the outside, and pink inside, or according to taste.

6 Sprinkle the noisettes with salt and pepper and serve with mâche and a dollop of the Pink Peppercorn Butter Sauce.

ITALIAN BREAST OF LAMB

This recipe serves 6–8.

INGREDIENTS

3lb (1.5kg) breast of lamb
2 garlic bulbs, cloves separated and finely chopped
3 tbsp dried mixed herbs
3 tbsp balsamic vinegar, plus extra for sprinkling
¼ cup (60ml) olive oil
salt and black pepper
1 fennel bulb, cut into bite-sized chunks, to garnish

PREPARATION

1 Score the fatty side of the lamb, then rub the meat all over with garlic, herbs, vinegar, and olive oil and sprinkle generously with salt and pepper. Wrap in plastic wrap and marinate for at least 3 hours, or overnight in the refrigerator.
2 Prepare a charcoal fire or preheat a gas grill.
3 Cook the lamb over low heat, preferably covered, for 1–1½ hours, turning once or twice, until the meat is crisply browned on the outside and much of the fat has been rendered.
4 Serve hot, sprinkled with balsamic vinegar and garnished with chunks of fennel.

MEAT PATTIES STUFFED WITH FETA

INGREDIENTS

1lb (500g) lean ground lamb or beef
5 shallots, finely chopped
5 garlic cloves, finely chopped
3oz (90g) feta, sliced
salt and black pepper
Crisp Salad
½ cucumber, diced
1 red pepper, cored, seeded, and diced
2–3 handfuls of mâche, arugula, or other greens
2 ripe tomatoes, diced
Classic Vinaigrette (see page 44)

PREPARATION

1 Combine the meat in a bowl with the shallots and garlic. Form into 4 patties, then halve each one horizontally. Pat them out until thin. Cover 4 patties with slices of feta, then top with the other 4 halves. Pinch the edges to seal, then season.
2 Prepare a charcoal fire or preheat a gas grill.
3 Cook the patties over hot coals, preferably covered, for 3–4 minutes or until browned, then turn to cook the other side.
4 Toss the salad ingredients in a bowl. Top each patty with some salad and serve immediately.

BUTTERFLIED LEG OF LAMB

This is a classic technique: the boned leg of lamb is laid out flat so that it cooks evenly. Skewers help keep the meat flat and make it easy to handle while cooking. It is important not to overcook the meat: serve it browned and slightly charred on the outside, pink and juicy inside. This recipe serves 6–8.

INGREDIENTS

1 leg of lamb, about 5lb (2.5kg)
handful of rosemary sprigs
1½ garlic bulbs, cloves separated and cut into large slivers
1 cup (250ml) red wine, plus extra if necessary
⅓ cup (90ml) olive oil
salt and black pepper

PREPARATION

1 Prepare the leg of lamb (see steps, right). Remove any remaining skin or excess fat and lay the boned lamb on a board, skin side down.
2 Make 10–20 small incisions all over the meat with a sharp knife and insert a small sprig of rosemary and a sliver of garlic in each slit, using about half the rosemary and garlic. Lay the meat out flat in a large shallow dish. Pour the red wine over the meat, then marinate at room temperature for at least 1 hour.
3 Prepare a charcoal fire or preheat a gas grill.
4 Remove the meat from the marinade and pat dry with paper towels. Use 4 long skewers to hold the meat flat in the "butterfly" position while it is cooking.
5 Finely chop the remaining rosemary and garlic, mix with the olive oil, and brush half over the lamb. Season with salt and pepper.
6 Place a drip pan under the grill (see page 147) and pour in about 1 cup (250ml) water. Place the skewered lamb on the grill and cook over hot coals for about 20 minutes on each side, covered if possible. Turn the meat from time to time and baste with the remaining olive oil mixture. The lamb is done when it is brown and charred on the outside, but still pink or rosy pink inside, according to taste. The total cooking time will be 35–40 minutes.
7 Place the lamb on a board and let rest for about 10 minutes. Pour the liquid from the drip pan into a small saucepan. Skim off the fat and boil the liquid to reduce it if the gravy is thin. If the gravy is thick and concentrated, thin it with a little wine.
8 Slice the lamb thin and pour on the gravy. Serve with Red Onion and Raisin Relish (see page 128) and chargrilled green beans.

BUTTERFLYING A LEG OF LAMB

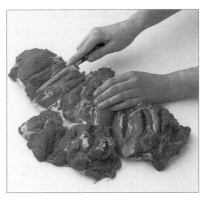

1 Cut around the shank (lower leg) bone with a sharp knife, then scrape the meat away from the bone until you expose the joint with the upper leg bone.

2 Continue to scrape the meat away from the leg bone. Sever the thread-like tendons and ease both bones out, cutting and scraping the meat away.

3 Open out the meat and make deep cuts in any thick portions so that it lies flat and is of even thickness all over. Remove any remaining tendons.

MOROCCAN LAMB BROCHETTES

This is consummate Moroccan street fare, cooked while you wait and best eaten immediately, while still hot. Serve with pieces of French bread and slices of tomato, and perhaps a salad of mixed herbs and olives.

INGREDIENTS

1½lb (750g) boneless shoulder chops,
cut into bite-sized pieces
1 onion, finely chopped
5 garlic cloves, finely chopped
2 tsp crumbled dried bay leaves or herbes de Provence
pinch of dried thyme
2 tsp ground cumin
½ tsp turmeric
juice of 1½ lemons
⅓ cup (90ml) olive oil
salt and black pepper
1 tbsp paprika
1 tbsp chopped fresh cilantro

PREPARATION

1 Place the lamb in a shallow dish with the onion, garlic, bay leaves or herbes de Provence, thyme, half the cumin, the turmeric, lemon juice, and olive oil. Mix well, then marinate for at least 30 minutes and up to 3 hours at room temperature, or overnight in the refrigerator.
2 Prepare a charcoal fire or preheat a gas grill. Get 8 skewers ready – wooden skewers should be soaked in cold water for 30 minutes.
3 Thread the lamb onto the skewers, then season to taste. Cook over hot coals until browned on one side, about 5 minutes, then turn and cook the other side. Be careful not to overcook.
4 Serve the kebabs immediately, sprinkled with the remaining cumin, the paprika, and cilantro.

FILLET OF BEEF

Cooking a whole or half fillet of beef is a rare treat, so long as it is not overdone. This is one of the most spectacular dishes I have barbecued, all the more remarkable for its simplicity. If you like, have the butcher trim the fillet closely and cut it into "roasts," which will be easier to cook on the grill – reduce the cooking time accordingly. This serves 4–6.

INGREDIENTS

2–3lb (1–1.5kg) fillet of beef, fat trimmed
1 cup (250ml) dry red wine
1 onion, chopped
2 garlic cloves, finely chopped
½ cup (125ml) olive oil
salt and black pepper

PREPARATION

1 Place the beef fillet in a shallow dish with the wine, onion, garlic, and half the olive oil. Turn to coat well, then marinate at room temperature for up to 3 hours.
2 Prepare a charcoal fire or preheat a gas grill.
3 Remove the fillet from the marinade and rub well with the remaining olive oil.
4 Cook, preferably covered, until the meat is browned but still rare inside, or according to taste. Turn several times so that the fillet cooks evenly. It should take about 20 minutes and have a bit of "give" when pressed with the finger, but feel slightly firm. Test with a metal skewer to check that the color of the juices is to your taste.
5 Remove the beef from the grill and let rest on a board for 10 minutes, to let the juices settle, before slicing. Serve sprinkled with salt and pepper, accompanied by fettuccine tossed with Roquefort, crème fraîche, shallots, and pine nuts.

FAJITAS

Fajitas come from the border between Texas and Mexico. The name means "little belt" and refers to a specific cut of meat, skirt steak, though chicken and spicy sausages are often included in the dish. Fajitas are served with tortillas, Guacamole (see page 126), Salsa (see page 124), Refried Beans (see page 132), and sour cream.

INGREDIENTS

½lb (250g) skirt steak or other tender steak
Mexican Chili Paste (see page 41)
4 tbsp tequila
1 chicken breast, boned but not skinned
2 chorizo sausages, poached, optional
3–4 small onions, unpeeled and halved lengthwise
2 ripe plantains, peeled and halved lengthwise
12 flour tortillas
1 red chili, finely chopped
sliced limes, cilantro, and shredded lettuce,
to garnish

PREPARATION

1 Spread the steak with half the chili paste and let stand for 10 minutes. Sprinkle on 2 tablespoons of the tequila, then cover and marinate in the refrigerator overnight, or up to 2 days.
2 Spread the chicken breast with the rest of the chili paste and sprinkle with the remaining tequila. Refrigerate for 1–2 hours.
3 Prepare a charcoal fire or preheat a gas grill.
4 Cook the steak over hot coals for 8–10 minutes, turning once or twice, until it is done on the outside and still rare inside, or to taste.
5 When the steak is half cooked, add the chicken and cook for about 4 minutes on each side, or until the juices run clear when pierced with a skewer. Do not overcook. Add the poached sausages, if using, onions, and plantains, and grill for 2–3 minutes on each side.
6 Sprinkle each tortilla with a little cold water, then heat for 30 seconds or so on each side. Keep warm in a clean dish towel. Alternatively, sprinkle the tortillas with a little water, then wrap in foil and place on the coolest part of the barbecue for about 5 minutes.
7 Remove the onions and plantains and place on a serving platter. Cut the steak and chicken into thin strips and slice the sausages. Arrange the meats on the platter and sprinkle with the chopped chili. Serve with the tortillas, Guacamole (see page 126), Salsa (see page 124), Refried Beans (see page 132), and sour cream. Garnish with sliced limes, cilantro leaves, and shredded lettuce.

RATTLESNAKE JUNCTION BARBECUED STEAK

Cooked over an open fire, this is hearty fare from America's cowboy heartland. I like it best accompanied by thick slices of grilled onion and a tomato salad, with potatoes baked in the ashes. The zesty marinade is best used on tougher cuts of meat that need some tenderizing.

INGREDIENTS

2lb (1kg) rump, chuck, or flank steak
Rattlesnake Junction Marinade
2 tbsp paprika
4 garlic cloves, finely chopped
½ cup (125ml) beer
2 tbsp soy sauce
1 tsp dried thyme
2 tsp Dijon mustard
juice of ½ lemon

PREPARATION

1 To make the marinade, mix the paprika with the garlic, beer, soy sauce, thyme, mustard, and lemon, then spread it over both sides of the steak.
2 Place the steak in a shallow dish and marinate at room temperature for 3 hours, or covered in the refrigerator for up to 6 hours.
3 Prepare a charcoal fire or preheat a gas grill.
4 Cook the steak over hot coals, turning once or twice, until it is just cooked through, but not overcooked, 8–10 minutes. It should be pink to red inside, to taste. Timing will vary according to its thickness.
5 Serve thinly sliced across the grain. Accompany with thickly sliced barbecued onions, a tomato salad, and baked potatoes.

STEAK JALISCO STYLE

This delicious steak is wonderfully simple: marinated in orange and olive oil and eaten rare, with a squeeze of lime and a sprinkling of cayenne.

INGREDIENTS

2 oranges, thinly sliced
4 tender beef steaks, such as sirloin or fillet,
½lb (250g) each
3 tbsp olive oil
salt and ground cayenne
lime wedges and red chilies, to garnish

PREPARATION

1 Arrange half the orange slices in a shallow dish. Lay the steaks on top, then cover with the remaining orange slices. Drizzle with half the olive oil and let stand for 1–3 hours.
2 Prepare a charcoal fire or preheat a gas grill.
3 Remove the steaks from the marinade and wipe dry. Rub lightly with olive oil, then cook quickly over hot coals for 8–10 minutes until just rare, or to taste, turning once or twice.
4 Sprinkle the steaks with salt and cayenne and serve immediately, garnished with lime wedges and red chilies. Serve with Salsa and Roasted Green Chili Salsa (see pages 124–25).

TUSCAN-STYLE STEAK

One of the glories of Tuscan cuisine, this steak dish is eaten drizzled with olive oil and lemon juice. Follow with ripe nectarines and a pungent cheese.

INGREDIENTS

4 tender beef steaks, such as sirloin or fillet,
½lb (250g) each
3–4 tbsp olive oil
pinch of dried sage or oregano
salt and black pepper
juice of 2 lemons

PREPARATION

1 Place the steaks in a shallow dish and pour over half the olive oil. Turn to coat, then sprinkle with the sage or oregano. Marinate at room temperature for up to 3 hours.
2 Prepare a charcoal fire or preheat a gas grill.
3 Cook over hot coals for 8–10 minutes, until brown but still rare inside, turning once or twice.
4 Remove the steaks and sprinkle with salt and pepper, then drizzle with the remaining olive oil and lemon juice to taste. Serve immediately.

ANTICUCHOS

The national dish of Peru, anticuchos were traditionally made from llamas' hearts. Today, however, they are more likely to be prepared from beef heart or tender steak.

INGREDIENTS

1 tbsp annatto seeds
½ cup (125ml) water
1 tbsp cumin seeds
4–5 garlic cloves, finely chopped
salt and black pepper
1 green or red chili, chopped
⅔ cup (175ml) red wine vinegar
2 tbsp olive oil
pinch of dried oregano or marjoram
1½lb (750g) sirloin or other tender steak,
cut into cubes
¼–½ tsp dried, crushed red chili flakes
8–12 small hot red chilies, optional

PREPARATION

1 Place the annatto seeds and water in a small pan. Bring to a boil, simmer for 2–3 minutes. then remove from the heat and leave the seeds overnight to soften. Alternatively, omit cooking and soaking and grind the seeds in a coffee grinder.
2 Toast the cumin seeds in a dry heavy skillet until fragrant, but not browned. Remove from the heat and crush in a mortar or spice grinder.
3 Purée the garlic with salt, then add the cumin, fresh chili, black pepper, vinegar, 1 tablespoon of olive oil, and the oregano. Mix well.
4 Place the steak in a shallow dish, spoon over half the cumin-garlic mixture, and turn to coat. Marinate for 2–3 hours.
5 Prepare a charcoal fire or preheat a gas grill. Get 8 skewers ready – wooden skewers should be soaked in cold water for 30 minutes.
6 Drain the annatto seeds, reserving the cooking water. Crush the seeds, then stir in the cooking water, crushed red chili, and the remaining olive oil. If using ground seeds, add ⅓ cup (90ml) water.
7 Heat the remaining marinade until it comes to a boil. Cook for 2–3 minutes, then remove from the heat and stir in the annatto mixture.
8 Thread the beef onto the skewers, adding 2–3 chilies if desired, then brush with some of the marinade mixture.
9 Cook over hot coals for 8–10 minutes until browned, turning once or twice, then brush again with the mixture. Serve with chargrilled sweet potatoes and corn on the cob, and a selection of relishes (see pages 128–29).

GEORGIAN SHISH KEBAB

Kebabs originated in the Caucasus, where legend has it they were served up on the point of a sword – the word kebab is actually Turkish. This style of cooking was then taken up by the Russians and Georgians, who prefer kebabs made from beef rather than lamb.

INGREDIENTS

1½lb (750g) sirloin or other beef, cut into bite-sized cubes
3–5 garlic cloves, finely chopped
1 small onion, chopped
10 black peppercorns, coarsely ground
1 cup (250ml) red wine
handful of fresh bay leaves
3 small onions, cut into wedges
3 green peppers, cored, seeded, and cut into wedges
½ cup (125ml) sunflower oil
salt and black pepper
lemon slices and pickled red peppers, to garnish

PREPARATION

1 Place the beef in a shallow dish with the garlic, onion, peppercorns, wine, and bay leaves. Turn to coat, then marinate for at least 3 hours and up to 8 hours at room temperature, or overnight in the refrigerator.

2 Prepare a charcoal fire or preheat a gas grill. Get 8 skewers ready – wooden skewers should be soaked in cold water for 30 minutes.

3 Thread the meat and bay leaves onto the skewers, alternating with wedges of onion and pepper. Push the pieces tightly together on the skewers and brush with oil.

4 Cook over hot coals, turning occasionally and basting with oil as needed. Allow 5–7 minutes for rare kebabs, 9–10 minutes for medium-rare, and 12–13 minutes for medium. Be careful not to overcook the kebabs.

5 Serve immediately, sprinkled with salt and pepper and garnished with lemon slices and pickled red chili peppers.

Steak Jalisco Style
(see page 100)

Jerk Pork Ribs
(see page 105)

*Roasted Green
Chili Salsa
(see page 125)*

*Anticuchos
(see page 100)*

STEAK & MUSHROOMS WITH ROASTED GARLIC BUTTER

When you are ready to barbecue, slather some of the butter on the steaks and set them on the hot grill. When they are ready, slightly charred on the outside, rare within, top with a little more of the butter to melt into a sauce. Accompany with tender-crisp young string beans, and ripe cheese and fruit for dessert.

INGREDIENTS

4 sirloin or fillet steaks, 6–8oz (175–250g) each
1 cup (250ml) red wine
4 large brown mushrooms or a selection of wild mushrooms, such as oyster, shiitake, morels, porcini, chanterelles
2 tbsp finely chopped fresh parsley
Roasted Garlic Butter
5 garlic cloves, finely chopped
¼ tsp salt
15 roasted garlic cloves, flesh squeezed out (see page 152)
¾ cup (175g) butter
salt and black pepper

PREPARATION

1 Place the steaks in a shallow dish, pour on the wine, and marinate for 1–3 hours at room temperature, turning occasionally.
2 Meanwhile, to make the butter, purée the raw garlic with the salt, then add the roasted garlic flesh and the butter and purée until it forms a smooth paste. Season with salt and pepper.
3 Prepare a charcoal fire or preheat a gas grill.
4 Remove the steaks from the wine; they will have absorbed much if not all of it. Pat dry with paper towels and spread both sides with a layer of the garlic butter. You should have half the butter left.
5 Cook over hot coals for 8–10 minutes, turning once or twice, until the outside is lightly charred and the inside is still rare, or to taste.
6 When the steaks are half cooked, thread the mushrooms onto skewers and spread with a little of the remaining butter. Place on the grill and cook for a few minutes on each side.
7 Serve the steaks and mushrooms spread with the rest of the garlic butter, so it melts enticingly on top, and sprinkle with chopped parsley.

KOREAN BEEF OR LAMB

Both the beef ribs and breast of lamb are fatty enough to baste themselves as they cook slowly. A few days marinating in spicy sauce (vary the heat to taste) produces meat that is juicy and delicious.

INGREDIENTS

2lb (1kg) beef short ribs or breast of lamb
½ cup (125ml) soy sauce
¼ cup (60ml) sherry or sake
2 tbsp sesame oil
2 scallions, thinly sliced
2 tbsp sugar
¼ tsp ground cayenne, or to taste
5 garlic cloves, finely chopped
2 tsp chopped fresh ginger
6 tbsp toasted sesame seeds

PREPARATION

1 Place the meat in a shallow dish with the other ingredients. Turn to coat and marinate, covered, for 1–3 days in the refrigerator.
2 Prepare a charcoal fire or preheat a gas grill.
3 Cook the meat, covered if possible, over indirect heat (see page 147), turning occasionally, until it is brown and tender, about 35 minutes. Serve immediately with steamed rice sprinkled with scallions, and kimchi.

STEAK ALLA MEXICANA

INGREDIENTS

4 corn tortillas
½lb (250g) mild white cheese, grated
4 small steaks such as sirloin, ¼lb (125g) each
olive oil for brushing
salt and black pepper
Chipotle Salsa (see page 77)
1 tbsp chopped fresh cilantro

PREPARATION

1 Sprinkle the tortillas with a layer of cheese.
2 Brush the steaks with olive oil, then sprinkle with salt and pepper.
3 Prepare a charcoal fire or preheat a gas grill.
4 Cook the steaks over hot coals, covered if possible, for 3 minutes, then turn. Add the tortillas and cook until the steaks are browned, but still rare, and the cheese has melted. A cover will keep the meat juicy and help the cheese melt.
5 Place each steak on a cheese-topped tortilla, then spoon over Chipotle Salsa to cover the steak. Sprinkle with cilantro and serve immediately.

CHAR SIU-STYLE PORK

INGREDIENTS

½ cup (125ml) hoisin sauce
4 tbsp ketchup
2 tbsp soy sauce
¼ tsp crushed Szechuan peppercorns, toasted
¼ tsp five-spice powder
⅛ tsp ground cumin
2 tbsp honey
4 boneless pork chops, 6–8oz (175–250g) each
3 scallions, thinly sliced
2 tbsp chopped cashew nuts, toasted

PREPARATION

1 Mix the hoisin, ketchup, soy sauce, Szechuan peppercorns, five-spice powder, cumin, and half the honey in a shallow dish. Add the pork and turn until it is well coated. Marinate for up to 3 hours at room temperature or in the refrigerator overnight.
2 Prepare a charcoal fire or preheat a gas grill.
3 Remove the meat from the marinade and drain. Drizzle on the remaining honey, then cook over medium coals, turning once, until the chops are just cooked through, about 15 minutes.
4 Serve thinly sliced, sprinkled with the scallions and cashews.

GREEK PORK CHOPS

INGREDIENTS

3lb (1.5kg) pork chops or spareribs
1 onion, finely chopped
3 garlic cloves, chopped
½ cup (125ml) lemon juice
½ cup (125ml) olive oil
1 tsp dried oregano or mixed herbs
salt and black pepper
olives, parsley, and lemon wedges, to garnish

PREPARATION

1 Place the pork in a shallow dish with the onion, garlic, lemon juice, olive oil, oregano, salt, and pepper. Turn to coat, then marinate for at least 3 hours at room temperature or overnight in the refrigerator.
2 Prepare a charcoal fire or preheat a gas grill.
3 Remove the meat from the marinade and drain. Cook over medium-hot coals for about 8 minutes, preferably covered, until browned on one side, then turn and cook the other side.
4 Serve hot, sprinkled with salt and pepper and garnished with olives, parsley, and lemon wedges.

JERK PORK RIBS

"Jerk" is the Caribbean term for a very hot, spicy marinade. Jerk meat, marinated and cooked over the fire, is sold throughout Jamaica, in posh restaurants and from ramshackle street carts alike.

INGREDIENTS

2lb (1kg) pork spareribs
Caribbean Jerk
1 onion, finely chopped
2 tbsp lemon or lime juice
⅓ cup (90ml) olive oil
1 green chili, chopped
2 tbsp ground allspice
5 garlic cloves, finely chopped
½ tsp dried thyme
½ tsp crushed, dried red chilies
½ tsp freshly ground nutmeg
1 tsp chopped fresh ginger
salt and black pepper
¼ cup (60ml) rum
3 tbsp dark brown sugar
10–15 bay leaves

PREPARATION

1 Combine all the jerk ingredients in a shallow dish. Add the ribs and turn to coat, then cover and marinate overnight in the refrigerator.
2 Prepare a charcoal fire or preheat a gas grill.
3 Drain the pork and place on the barbecue. Remove the bay leaves from the marinade and scatter on the grill around the pork.
4 Cook the ribs slowly, preferably covered, until they are cooked through, 35–45 minutes, and are crusty and browned. Brush with oil occasionally if very lean. Serve immediately.

VARIATION

JERK PORK WITH GUAVA-APPLE RELISH Instead of ribs, use a boneless cut of pork, cut into bite-sized chunks and threaded on skewers. Cook for 5 minutes on each side, or until crusty and brown, and serve with Guava-Apple Relish (see page 128).

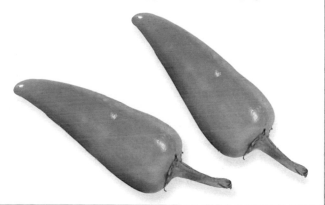

THAI-INSPIRED PORK

Make a double quantity of the spice paste for other uses: thinned with a little vinegar and sweetened with a bit more sugar, it makes a splendid dressing for thinly sliced cabbage, corn kernels, and shredded carrots.

INGREDIENTS

1½lb (750g) lean pork, cut into medallions
½ cup (125ml) sherry, port, or rice wine
½ cup (125ml) chicken stock
2 tbsp brown sugar
2–3 tbsp lime juice
Thai Spice Paste
2 tbsp grated fresh ginger
2 tbsp medium sherry, port, or rice wine
½ cup (60g) roasted peanuts, chopped or coarsely crushed
4 scallions, thinly sliced
1 tbsp each vegetable oil and sesame oil
1 green or red chili, finely chopped
1½ tsp turmeric
1 tbsp brown sugar
1 tbsp balsamic or raspberry vinegar
2 tsp ground cumin
1 medium bunch fresh cilantro, chopped
salt and black pepper

PREPARATION

1 Blend the Thai spice ingredients together to make a paste (if the nuts are salted, you may not need any extra salt, depending on taste).
2 Rub about half the paste on the pork medallions and leave for 1–3 hours at room temperature or overnight in the refrigerator.
3 Remove the meat from the marinade with a slotted spoon. Place the marinade in a saucepan with the sherry, chicken stock, sugar, and half the lime juice. Bring to a boil, then reduce the heat and cook until it forms an almost syrupy glaze.
4 Prepare a charcoal fire or preheat a gas grill.
5 Cook the pork over hot coals until charred on each side but juicy inside. Since medallions are so thin, this will take only 2–3 minutes on each side.
6 To serve, add the remaining spice paste to the sauce, along with the rest of the lime juice. Warm through and place a few spoonfuls on each plate with several slices of barbecued pork medallions on top. Serve with Middle Eastern Pilaf wrapped in banana leaves (see pages 133 and 154) and Red Onion and Raisin Relish (see page 128).

VARIATION

THAI FILLET OF BEEF Coat thin slices of fillet with the Thai Spice Paste. Cook quickly over hot coals, so the meat is brown outside, but still rare inside.

Sesame oil

Roasted peanuts

Fresh ginger

Lime juice

Brown sugar

Chicken stock

Sherry

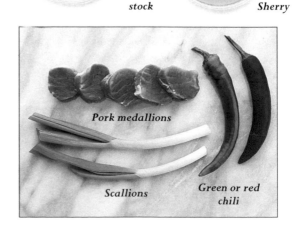

Pork medallions

Scallions

Green or red chili

Vegetable oil

Turmeric

Balsamic
vinegar

Ground
cumin

Cilantro

Salt

Black
pepper

PORK & GINGERED FRUIT

Use pork that is already smoked, so it can safely be
cooked with the sugary glaze, without fear of it burning.

INGREDIENTS

1½lb (750g) smoked pork loin, cut into chunks
Mango-Mustard Glaze (see page 41)
2–3 tbsp butter, softened
2 tbsp chopped preserved ginger, plus some of the syrup
ground ginger or grated fresh ginger, to taste
½ pineapple, peeled, sliced, and cut into chunks
2–4 ripe nectarines, pitted and cut into chunks
fresh mint sprigs, to garnish

Ginger Relish
4 tbsp chopped preserved ginger
3–4 dried apricots, diced
2 slices fresh pineapple, diced
2 tbsp chopped red chili
1 tbsp chopped fresh mint

PREPARATION

1 Place the pork in a shallow dish with the
Mango-Mustard Glaze and turn to coat well.
Marinate for 30–60 minutes.

2 Prepare a charcoal fire or preheat a gas grill.
Get 8 skewers ready – wooden skewers should be
soaked in cold water for 30 minutes.

3 Mix the butter with the preserved ginger and
syrup, and the ground or grated ginger. Spread the
butter on the fruit.

4 Remove the pork from the marinade and thread
the fruit and meat pieces alternately onto the
skewers. Cook the kebabs over hot coals,
preferably covered, turning once or twice until
lightly browned around the edges, about 4 minutes
on each side.

5 Mix together the Ginger Relish ingredients.
Serve the kebabs immediately with the relish and
garnish with mint sprigs. They are also good with
steamed rice and a crisp vegetable salad.

BRINE-CURED PORK ROAST WITH PORT & APPLE SAUCE

Curing meat in brine firms it up and slightly pickles it (see page 155 for curing instructions). This recipe serves 6–8.

INGREDIENTS

2 tbsp fennel seeds
½ tsp dried lavender
2 tsp herbes de Provence
zest of 1 orange
Brine (see page 155)
3lb (1.5kg) boneless pork roast
olive oil, for rubbing
8 apples, cut into thick slices
1 cup (250ml) meat stock
5–8 shallots, chopped
1 cup (250ml) port, or apple juice mixed with dry white wine
dash of raspberry vinegar, to taste
1 cup (250g) crème fraîche or light sour cream

PREPARATION

1 Add the fennel seeds, lavender, herbes de Provence, and orange zest to the other brine ingredients and prepare (see page 155). Let cool, then pour into a large glass bowl and add the pork. Cover and let steep in the refrigerator for 2 days.
2 Remove the meat from the brine and rinse well in several changes of water. Dry the pork on paper towels, then rub well all over with olive oil.
3 Prepare a charcoal fire or preheat a gas grill. Place a drip pan under the grill and half fill with water (see page 147).
4 Cook the pork, covered, over indirect heat with medium-hot coals for about 45 minutes, or until it is firm, cooked through, and lightly browned.
5 During the last 10 minutes, place the apple slices over a cooler part of the fire and cook until warmed through and tender.
6 Place the meat on a platter to rest, with half the apples. Skim off the fat from the drip pan liquid.
7 Dice the remaining apples and place in a skillet with the drip pan liquid, stock, shallots, and port. Bring to a boil and cook over high heat until reduced in volume by at least half.
8 Add the vinegar and any juices from the meat, boil for 1 minute, then stir in the crème fraîche and cook over medium-hot coals for another 5 minutes, or until the sauce thickens slightly.
9 Thinly slice the pork and add to the skillet with the sliced apples, stirring gently to warm through with the sauce. Serve with rice and mâche tossed in Classic Vinaigrette (see page 44).

BARBECUED VEAL CHOPS WITH WILD MUSHROOM SAUCE

This is a most luxurious dish, with a rich and elegant mushroom sauce.

INGREDIENTS

4 veal chops, preferably on the bone, 6–8oz (175–250g) each
5 garlic cloves, finely chopped
2 tbsp olive oil
juice of 1 lemon
1 tbsp chopped fresh rosemary
Wild Mushroom Sauce (see page 126)
chopped chives, to garnish

PREPARATION

1 Place the chops in a shallow dish with half the garlic, the olive oil, lemon juice, and rosemary. Marinate for 1–3 hours at room temperature or overnight in the refrigerator.
2 Prepare a charcoal fire or preheat a gas grill.
3 Cook the veal over hot coals for about 6 minutes on each side, or until the outside is lightly charred but the inside is still pink.
4 Serve the chops with the Wild Mushroom Sauce poured over and sprinkled with chives.

POUNDED VEAL WITH ROSEMARY-MUSTARD BUTTER

Veal, delicate and bland, is enhanced by the same gentle flavorings as chicken breast.

INGREDIENTS

4 veal scaloppines cut from the leg, about 6oz (175g) each
2 tbsp olive oil
juice of ½ lemon
salt and black pepper
Rosemary-Mustard Butter (see page 43)

PREPARATION

1 Place the veal between 2 sheets of waxed paper or plastic wrap or inside a plastic bag, and pound to ¼in (5mm) thickness.
2 Place the veal in a shallow dish with the olive oil, lemon juice, salt, and pepper, and turn to coat well. Marinate for 30–60 minutes.
3 Prepare a charcoal fire or preheat a gas grill.
4 Cook the veal quickly over hot coals for about 8 minutes, turning once or twice, until lightly charred but still pink inside. Spread with the flavored butter and serve immediately.

FIRE-ROASTED RABBIT WITH PANCETTA, HERBS, OLIVADA, & AIOLI

Rabbit is delicious cooked over an open fire, but since it is so lean, care must be taken to baste it with oil and, of course, not to overcook it.

INGREDIENTS

3 tbsp olive oil
1 tbsp lemon juice
1–2 tsp herbes de Provence
4 garlic cloves, finely chopped
salt and black pepper
1 rabbit, cut into serving pieces
6–8 slices of pancetta or bacon
2 tbsp fresh marjoram or oregano
¼ cup (60ml) black olive paste and Aïoli (see page 66)

PREPARATION

1 Mix together the olive oil, lemon juice, herbes de Provence, garlic, and seasoning. Rub the rabbit pieces all over with the mixture. Marinate for about an hour at room temperature.
2 Prepare a charcoal fire or preheat a gas grill.
3 Wrap the rabbit pieces in slices of pancetta, securing each piece with a bamboo skewer.
4 Cook over medium-hot coals for 30–35 minutes, turning several times and basting with any remaining marinade.
5 Serve immediately, sprinkled with marjoram and accompanied by a bowl of olive paste and another of Aïoli.

VARIATION

ROSEMARY-MUSTARD AIOLI Omit the olive paste. Add to the Aïoli 2–3 tablespoons chopped fresh rosemary and 1 tablespoon whole-grain mustard.

TURKEY SAUSAGES WITH CRANBERRY MUSTARD

Any kind of meaty herbed sausage is fine for this dish, but turkey sausage is especially good with the flavorful cranberry mustard. Only the very best quality sausages are worth barbecuing. For other relishes, see pages 128-29.

INGREDIENTS

1lb (500g) turkey sausages
1–2 tbsp Dijon mustard
3 tbsp cranberry sauce
1–2 tsp sugar, or to taste
½–1 tsp red wine or Berry Vinegar (see page 45)

PREPARATION

1 Prepare a charcoal fire or preheat a gas grill.
2 Cook the sausages over medium coals for 6–8 minutes on each side, or until golden brown.
3 Meanwhile, stir the mustard into the cranberry sauce, then stir in the sugar and vinegar.
4 Serve the sausages sizzling hot with the cranberry mustard.

WHITE SAUSAGES WITH PRUNES

White sausages, such as bratwurst, are delectable cooked on the fire. One of my recent favorites was truffle-scented boudin blanc, toted back from Paris.

INGREDIENTS

16 pitted prunes
2 cups (500ml) scalding hot black tea
2 tbsp butter, melted
4 white sausages, about 3oz (90g) each

PREPARATION

1 Steep the prunes in the tea until the tea has cooled and the prunes have plumped up, about 30 minutes.
2 Prepare a charcoal fire or preheat a gas grill. Get 4 skewers ready – wooden skewers should be soaked in cold water for 30 minutes.
3 Drain the prunes and thread onto the skewers. Brush with the melted butter and set aside.
4 Cook the sausages over medium-hot coals, turning occasionally, until cooked evenly to a light golden color, about 15 minutes.
5 When the sausages are half cooked, place the prunes on the barbecue and heat while the sausages finish cooking. Remove the prunes from the skewers and serve with the hot sausages.

SAUSAGE SELECTION

*Along with the usual pork or beef, try duck, game,
chicken, turkey, even seafood sausages. Different types
will have differing cooking times, depending on
thickness — cut into one to test.*

INGREDIENTS

*2lb (1kg) assorted sausages, such as smoked kielbasa,
Toulouse, merguez, chorizo, or bratwurst
4 onions, peeled and halved
3 peppers, red, yellow, and green, cored, seeded,
and halved
2 fennel bulbs, quartered lengthwise
2–3 tbsp olive oil
juice of ½ lemon
salt and black pepper
thyme sprigs, to garnish*

PREPARATION

1 Prepare a charcoal fire or preheat a gas grill.
2 Cook the sausages over medium coals. Turn
to cook evenly. Cut one to test after 10 minutes.
3 Toss the vegetables with oil and lemon juice,
and season. Add to the grill with the sausages.
4 As the individual sausages and vegetables are
cooked through, remove and keep warm.
5 Serve with a selection of relishes (see pages
128–29) and garnish with thyme.

VARIATION

NEW YORK SAUSAGE SANDWICH Choose
smoked kielbasa, knockwurst, or spicy or Italian
sausages. Omit the yellow pepper, fennel, and
thyme. When the onions and peppers are done,
cut into dice. Serve in hot crusty rolls with a
spoonful of onion-pepper relish.

BREADS & SNACKS

Dough baked over a wood or charcoal fire traditionally makes bread with a crisp crust and smoky scent (the best boulangeries in France bake in wood-burning ovens). Large thick loaves do not fare well on the barbecue, but pizzas and flat breads such as focaccia, tortillas, and pita are delicious cooked over the fire. So are bread and cheese kebabs, and the flat chick-pea crêpe known in Nice as *socca*.

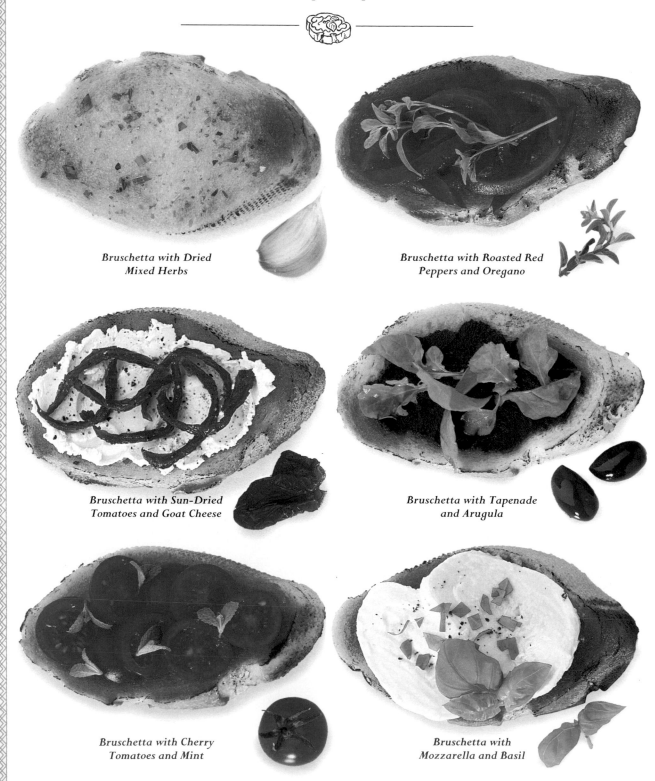

*Bruschetta with Dried
Mixed Herbs*

*Bruschetta with Roasted Red
Peppers and Oregano*

*Bruschetta with Sun-Dried
Tomatoes and Goat Cheese*

*Bruschetta with Tapenade
and Arugula*

*Bruschetta with Cherry
Tomatoes and Mint*

*Bruschetta with
Mozzarella and Basil*

BRUSCHETTA

Bruschetta is delicious. what could surpass the pure flavor of bread, toasted over the fire, rubbed with garlic, and anointed with rich olive oil. The roughness of the toasted surface acts like a grater, allowing the bread to pick up the strong flavor and scent of the garlic.

INGREDIENTS

4 thick slices country bread, such as ciabatta
4 garlic cloves, halved
extra-virgin olive oil, to taste
salt, to taste, optional

PREPARATION

1 Prepare a charcoal fire or preheat a gas grill.
2 Toast the bread slices on both sides over medium-hot coals until crisp and golden.
3 Rub both sides of each slice with the cut garlic. Drizzle with olive oil and serve. (If using traditional saltless Tuscan bread, sprinkle with salt.)
TOPPING SUGGESTIONS Dried and fresh herbs, roasted peppers, tomatoes, goat cheese, tapenade, arugula, and mozzarella are all delicious.

ROSEMARY-GARLIC BREAD

Crisped on the barbecue, this hot toasted bread makes an excellent appetizer: serve with a plate of spicy salami, fresh mozzarella, ripe garden tomatoes, and tangy green olives. It also makes a terrific base for a hot melted sandwich.

INGREDIENTS

10 garlic cloves, chopped
salt, to taste
2–3 tbsp chopped fresh rosemary
½ cup (125ml) olive oil
1 loaf country bread, such as ciabatta, split in half, then sliced into individual portions

PREPARATION

1 Purée the garlic with salt, preferably using a mortar and pestle, then add the rosemary and lightly crush into the garlic mixture.
2 Mix in the olive oil, then brush most of this mixture very generously onto the cut surfaces of the bread pieces.
3 Prepare a charcoal fire or preheat a gas grill.
4 Toast the bread on both sides over hot coals, until crisp and golden brown.
5 Remove from the heat and brush once again with the garlic-rosemary oil. Serve immediately.

BRUSCHETTA WITH SUN-DRIED TOMATOES & GOAT CHEESE

This open sandwich can also be topped with a salad of arugula leaves tossed in Classic Vinaigrette (see page 44).

INGREDIENTS

4 thick slices country bread, such as ciabatta
2 garlic cloves, halved
2 tbsp olive oil
¼lb (125g) mild goat cheese
8 sun-dried tomatoes, drained and sliced
black pepper

PREPARATION

1 Prepare a charcoal fire or preheat a gas grill.
2 Toast the bread on both sides over medium-hot coals until crisp and golden brown. Rub both sides of the bread with the cut garlic.
3 Drizzle or brush each garlic toast on one side with the olive oil, then spread with a layer of goat cheese. Arrange the strips of sun-dried tomato on top. Sprinkle with black pepper and serve.

TOSTADAS IBIZA

In a little hilltop village on the island of Ibiza is a bar-café that specializes in these garlicky toasted cheese and ham sandwiches. The café is filled with the sound of laughter and conversation, even passionate arguing, while always in the background is the call for just one more "tostada!"

INGREDIENTS

4 country bread rolls, such as ciabatta, cut open
¼–⅓ cup (60–90ml) olive oil
4 garlic cloves, halved
4 ripe tomatoes, halved
4 slices prosciutto, jamón, or other ham
4 thin slices Manchego or Gouda
1 tsp dried mixed herbs

PREPARATION

1 Prepare a charcoal fire or preheat a gas grill.
2 Brush the rolls generously with the olive oil and toast the cut sides over hot coals until they are golden brown and crunchy.
3 Rub the cut surface of each roll with the cut garlic. Arrange the halved tomatoes on each roll, then top with a slice each of ham and cheese. Sprinkle a little of the mixed herbs on the filling, then close the rolls.
4 Lightly toast the rolls on both sides until the cheese melts, then serve immediately.

PIZZA DOUGH

I keep several batches of this dough in the freezer. Once it has defrosted, the pizza is very easy to put together.

INGREDIENTS

1 envelope active dried yeast
3½ cups (425g) unbleached all-purpose flour
3 tbsp whole-wheat or rye flour
pinch of sugar
2 tsp salt
1 cup (250ml) warm water
olive oil for oiling bowl and dough

PREPARATION

1 Mix together the yeast, 3 cups of the all-purpose flour, the whole-wheat flour, sugar, and salt in a large bowl.
2 Stir in the water and mix well using a wooden spoon. When a stiff dough forms, turn out onto a floured board. Knead well, sprinkling the dough with the remaining flour as you work to keep it from sticking. Knead the dough for 5–8 minutes, or until it is elastic and smooth.
3 Place the dough in a large bowl coated with olive oil and rub oil over it. Cover with a clean cloth or plastic wrap and leave in a warm, draft-free place until doubled in size, about 1½–2 hours.
4 Punch down the dough with your knuckles to expel the air. (At this point the dough can be placed in a plastic bag and frozen. When ready to use, defrost and proceed to step 5.)
5 Knead the dough lightly for 1–2 minutes, then return to the oiled bowl, cover, and leave in a warm place to rise a second time, until it has again doubled in size, about 45 minutes.
6 Punch down the dough again, then roll or pat out on a large oiled baking sheet into 1 large pizza about 18in (45cm) across or 4 individual pizzas. Top as desired (see below), and bake over medium-hot coals. On an open barbecue the dough will need to be cooked on one side before adding the toppings (see page 116, step 3).

PIZZETTE WITH FIELD MUSHROOMS OR PORCINI

This makes 4 individual pizzas, slightly more elegant and less unwieldy than a large one. Smaller pizzas can be baked directly on the barbecue, as long as the grill is well oiled. If cooking on an open barbecue, see page 116.

INGREDIENTS

3oz (90g) dried or 6oz (175g) fresh cèpes, porcini, or other field mushrooms
1 recipe Pizza Dough (see left)
4 tbsp tomato paste
2 garlic cloves, finely chopped
½lb (250g) mozzarella, thinly sliced
½ cup (60g) freshly grated Parmesan or Pecorino
olive oil for drizzling

PREPARATION

1 Pour boiling water over the dried mushrooms, if using, and steep at room temperature for at least 30 minutes, or until softened. If using fresh mushrooms, simply slice them.
2 When the dried mushrooms are softened, drain and squeeze dry, reserving the soaking liquid. Cut off the hard stems.
3 Prepare a charcoal fire or preheat a gas grill.
4 Pat out the dough into 4 rounds. If cooking uncovered, see page 116, step 3, for instructions on precooking the base, then continue as below.
5 Spread the tomato paste over each round of dough, then arrange the mushrooms on top. Sprinkle with garlic, then top with slices of mozzarella and a sprinkling of Parmesan or Pecorino. Drizzle with 2 teaspoons of the mushroom soaking liquid and with olive oil.
6 Bake the pizzas directly on the grill or on an oiled baking sheet over medium-hot coals, covered if using a covered barbecue.
7 Cook until the dough has puffed up and turned golden brown, and the cheese has melted, 10–15 minutes. Serve hot.

TOPPINGS FOR BARBECUED PIZZA

Most favorite pizza toppings are even more delicious on a barbecue-cooked pizza.

INGREDIENTS

grilled eggplant slices, roasted tomatoes, and artichoke hearts; or
sun-dried tomatoes, basil, and kernels of corn; or
grilled radicchio, mozzarella, and pine nuts; or
Pesto (see page 124); or
prosciutto and artichoke hearts; or
spicy lamb meatballs and mushrooms; or
roasted green peppers and ricotta; or
fresh herbs, prosciutto, garlic, and freshly grated Parmesan or Pecorino; or
sliced red onions, capers, and sliced Fontina; or
a selection of barbecued vegetables (see page 10)

DOUBLE GARLIC PIZZA

There is a little restaurant in New York's Greenwich Village that is famous for its garlic pizza. For years, this has been my last stop before the airport; whether heading east to Europe or west to California, the infusion of garlic fortifies me for the rigors of the journey.

INGREDIENTS

1 recipe Pizza Dough (see page 114)
¾ cup (175ml) tomato pizza sauce
8–10 garlic cloves, finely chopped
2 tbsp chopped fresh parsley
large pinch of dried Italian herbs
½lb (250g) mozzarella, thinly sliced
freshly grated Parmesan or Pecorino
olive oil for drizzling
Garlic-Oil Condiment
5–8 garlic cloves, finely chopped
¼ cup (60ml) olive oil

PREPARATION

1 Prepare a charcoal fire or preheat a gas grill.
2 Roll or pat out the dough on a large oiled baking sheet to make 1 large pizza about 18in (45cm) across. If cooking uncovered, see page 116, step 3, for instructions on precooking the base, then continue as below.
3 Spread the top with tomato pizza sauce, then sprinkle with the garlic, parsley, and herbs. Top with the mozzarella and grated Parmesan or Pecorino, and drizzle with olive oil.
4 Place the pizza over medium-hot coals and cover if using a covered barbecue. Cook until the dough has puffed up and turned golden brown, and the cheese has melted, 10–15 minutes.
5 Meanwhile, make the Garlic-Oil Condiment by combining the garlic and olive oil. For a mellower, less harsh flavor, heat gently until the first bubbles appear at the edge of the pan, then remove from the heat immediately.
6 Serve the pizza hot, drizzled with the garlic-flavored oil.

VARIATION

When ripe sweet tomatoes are in season, they make a delicious and colorful topping. Place slices of tomato on top of the mozzarella, then sprinkle with the Parmesan or Pecorino. The tomatoes will roast as the pizza bakes.

ASPARAGUS PIZZA

From the moment I first tasted this, bought from a pizzeria in Florence one spring afternoon, it has been a favorite. It is simple to prepare and as comforting as it is lively. The Asparagus & Tomato Sauce should be prepared ahead of time, so that it is cool when spread on the dough.

INGREDIENTS

1 recipe Pizza Dough (see page 114)
handful of fresh basil leaves, thinly sliced
½lb (250g) mozzarella, thinly sliced
olive oil for drizzling
½ cup (60g) freshly grated Parmesan or Pecorino, plus extra to serve
crushed dried red chilies, to taste
Asparagus & Tomato Sauce
2 tbsp olive oil
6 garlic cloves, finely chopped
1lb (500g) asparagus, ends trimmed and cut into bite-sized pieces
2lb (1kg) tomatoes, fresh or canned, chopped
salt and black pepper
sugar, to taste

PREPARATION

1 Prepare a charcoal fire or preheat a gas grill.
2 First make the sauce. Gently heat the olive oil in a pan, add the garlic, and warm over low heat until its aroma is released but the garlic is not browned. Add the asparagus and cook for 2–3 minutes in the garlic oil.
3 Add the tomatoes, salt, pepper, and sugar, and cook over high heat until the tomatoes form a chunky sauce. Let cool.
4 Roll or pat out the dough on a large oiled baking sheet to make 1 large pizza about 18in (45cm) across or 4 individual pizzas. If cooking uncovered, see page 116, step 3, for instructions on precooking the base, then continue as below.
5 Spread the top with the sauce, distributing the asparagus pieces evenly over the pizza. Sprinkle with basil, arrange the mozzarella slices on top, then drizzle with olive oil and sprinkle with Parmesan or Pecorino.
6 Place the pizza over medium-hot coals and cover if using a covered barbecue. Individual pizzas can be baked directly on the oiled grill.
7 Cook until the dough has puffed up and turned golden brown, and the cheese has melted, 10–15 minutes. Serve immediately, sprinkled with extra Parmesan cheese and crushed dried red chilies, to taste.

MEDITERRANEAN PIZZA

*Olive paste and a generous helping of garlic make
this pizza deliciously zesty. Serve with a green
salad tossed with Classic Vinaigrette (see page 44),
and a glass of Valpolicella or Zinfandel.*

INGREDIENTS

1 recipe Pizza Dough (see page 114)
⅔ cup (150g) tomato paste
6 garlic cloves, finely chopped
3–4 tbsp cooked, chopped spinach, squeezed dry
¼ cup (75g) black olive paste
4 black olives
1–2 tsp dried mixed herbs or thyme
4–5 sun-dried tomatoes in oil, diced, optional
7oz (200g) feta, thinly sliced
½lb (250g) mozzarella, shredded
2 tbsp olive oil

PREPARATION

1 Prepare a charcoal fire, or preheat a gas grill.
2 Roll or pat out the dough on a large oiled
baking sheet to make 1 large pizza about 18in
(45cm) in diameter. If using a covered barbecue,
go to step 4.
3 If using an uncovered barbecue, you need to
cook the pizza base on one side first before adding
the topping. Place the pizza base on the baking
sheet over medium-hot coals and cook for 3–4
minutes, until the dough is lightly golden
underneath. Remove from the heat and turn the
pizza base over, so that the cooked side is
uppermost.
4 Spread the pizza with the tomato paste, then
sprinkle with the chopped garlic. Dot with the
cooked spinach and the olive paste, then sprinkle
with the olives, herbs, and sun-dried tomatoes, if
using. Layer the feta and mozzarella on top, then
drizzle with the olive oil.
5 Place the pizza over medium-hot coals, cover if
using a covered barbecue, and cook until the
topping has melted and turned lightly golden in
places, and the dough has puffed up and turned
golden brown, 10–15 minutes.

VARIATION

ARTICHOKE, SAUSAGE, & OLIVE PIZZETTE Pat out
the dough into 4 individual rounds on an oiled
baking sheet. Follow step 4 above, but replace the
spinach with 2 artichoke hearts, sliced and
blanched, and add 2 spicy pork or lamb sausages,
cut into bite-sized pieces. Arrange the artichoke
and sausage pieces on top of the cheese before
placing on the grill.

Black olives

Spinach

Garlic

Tomato paste

Pizza dough

Mixed herbs

Sun-Dried tomatoes

Feta

Mozzarella

Olive oil

Olive paste

CRISP-CRUSTED FLAT BREADS

INGREDIENTS

4 cups (500g) unbleached bread flour or
all-purpose flour
1 envelope active dried yeast
1 tsp salt
2 tbsp vegetable or olive oil, plus extra
for oiling and drizzling
1–1¼ cups (250–300ml) warm water

PREPARATION

1 Mix all the ingredients together in a bowl, using enough of the water to give a pliable dough, then turn on to a floured board and knead for 5 minutes or until the dough is smooth and elastic.
2 Place in an oiled bowl, cover, and leave in a warm place for at least 1 hour, until the dough has doubled in size. Punch down the dough. (At this point it can be wrapped in plastic wrap and frozen. When ready to use, defrost and proceed to step 3.)
3 Knead the dough lightly, then roll into balls the size of large eggs. Flatten the balls, then roll out into rounds 3–4in (7–10cm) in diameter and about ¼in (5mm) thick. Cover and leave in a warm place until doubled in size, about 40 minutes.
4 Prepare a charcoal fire or preheat a gas grill.
5 Place the rounds on the oiled grill over hot coals. Cover and bake for 5–8 minutes, or until the dough puffs up and turns golden brown.
6 Serve immediately with a Flavored Butter (see pages 42–43) or drizzled with olive oil.

VARIATIONS

SWEET RAISIN FOCACCIA Knead 3 tablespoons of sugar and 2–3 handfuls of raisins into the dough. Roll out, sprinkle with sugar, and bake as above.
ROSEMARY FOCACCIA Knead 2–3 tablespoons of chopped rosemary into the dough. Rub with olive oil, roll out flat, sprinkle with coarse salt, and bake as above. Serve with crushed garlic and olive oil.
FOCACCIA AUX LARDONS Knead 1¼ cups (250g) of diced salt pork or diced bacon (lardons) into the dough. Roll out and bake as above.
HERB-PECAN FOCACCIA Roll out the dough as directed. Sprinkle with herbes de Provence, chopped fresh rosemary, and 2–3 tablespoons of coarsely chopped pecans, then press into the dough with a rolling pin. Drizzle with olive oil and bake until lightly browned and puffed.
BULGARIAN CHEESE & ONION FLAT BREADS Knead 2 chopped onions and 1 cup (250g) grated Cheddar into the dough. Roll out as directed, then press in 1½ cups (175g) crumbled feta with a rolling pin. Bake until puffed and lightly golden.

SOCCA

Serve this Niçoise crêpe with Aïoli (see page 66).

INGREDIENTS

2 cups (250g) chick-pea flour
1 tbsp coarse salt
2 cups (500ml) water
pinch of herbes de Provence or thyme
olive oil for cooking

PREPARATION

1 Mix the chick-pea flour and salt, then stir in half the water, stirring until the lumps dissolve. Add more water until the mixture has the consistency of light cream. Add the dried herbs.
2 Let the mixture stand for at least 30 minutes. Stir well before using.
3 Prepare a charcoal fire or preheat a gas grill.
4 Heat a crêpe pan over hot coals, then add 1–2 tablespoons of oil to coat the pan. Heat until smoking, then remove from the heat and pour in enough batter to form a layer ¼in (5mm) thick.
5 Cook over hot coals, preferably covered so that both sides cook at once, about 10 minutes. The edges should be brown, even a little scorched, and the top set rather than liquid, with brown spots.
6 Repeat with the remaining batter. Serve sliced.

QUESADILLAS

INGREDIENTS

4 green bell peppers, roasted, peeled, cored,
and sliced (see page 54)
2 garlic cloves, finely chopped
1 hot green chili, such as jalapeño, chopped
salt and black pepper
3 tbsp olive oil
1 tbsp white vinegar
8 flour or corn tortillas
½ cup (125g) goat cheese, crumbled
½ cup (125g) mozzarella, grated

PREPARATION

1 Slice the peppers, place in a bowl with the garlic, chili, salt, pepper, 2 tablespoons of oil, and the vinegar, and marinate for 30 minutes.
2 Prepare a charcoal fire or preheat a gas grill.
3 Brush the tortillas with the remaining oil and heat on the grill for 1–2 minutes.
4 Spoon peppers, goat cheese, and mozzarella onto each tortilla. Fold into half-moons. Cook over hot coals until the cheese has melted, 2–3 minutes. Serve hot.

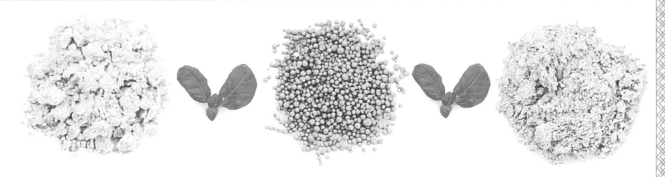

HALLOUMI, TOMATO, & BAY LEAF KEBABS

See illustration on page 19. These make terrific appetizers: full of flavor and very fresh-tasting. Halloumi toughens as it cools, so eat right away.

INGREDIENTS

3–4 large tomatoes, each cut into 8 chunks
½lb (250g) halloumi, cut into 24 chunks
3 garlic cloves, finely chopped
3 tbsp olive oil
24 bay leaves, preferably fresh

PREPARATION

1 Prepare a charcoal fire or preheat a gas grill. Get 8 skewers ready – wooden skewers should be soaked in cold water for 30 minutes.
2 Place the tomatoes and halloumi on a plate or in a shallow dish. Sprinkle with garlic and olive oil, then leave for 10–15 minutes.
3 Thread the tomatoes, halloumi, and bay leaves on the skewers, allowing about 3 bay leaves, 3 chunks of cheese, and 3 pieces of tomato per skewer. Save any garlic and olive oil left on the plate to season the hot barbecued kebabs.
4 Cook over hot coals for about 3 minutes on each side, preferably covered. Serve immediately, sprinkled with any leftover garlic and olive oil.

SPIEDINI

These bread and cheese kebabs are traditional to Rome.

INGREDIENTS

½ loaf (175g) slightly stale French bread, cut into chunks
½lb (250g) mozzarella or Cheddar, cut into chunks
½ cup (100g) Pesto (see page 124)
1 garlic clove, finely chopped
3 tbsp olive oil
2 red bell peppers, roasted, peeled, cored, and diced (see page 54)
2 tbsp white vinegar

PREPARATION

1 Prepare a charcoal fire or preheat a gas grill. Get 8 skewers ready – wooden skewers should be soaked in cold water for 30 minutes.
2 Thread the bread and cheese onto skewers, starting and ending with bread. Push the bread tightly onto the cheese so that it holds it in place.
3 Combine the Pesto with the garlic and olive oil.
4 Lay the skewers on a piece of foil and brush lightly with a little of the Pesto mixture.
5 Place the foil over medium-hot coals, preferably covered, so that the heat from the top toasts the bread as it cooks.
6 Cook for 8–10 minutes, turning if not covered, until the bread is toasted and the cheese has melted. Mix the remaining Pesto mixture with the diced peppers and vinegar and serve with the kebabs. If the cheese sticks to the foil, scrape it up carefully and place it back on the Spiedini.

TOPINKA

Topinka comes, I believe, from the Czech Republic. Its main ingredients are rye bread and garlic – the cheese can be varied at will.

INGREDIENTS

4 thick slices rye bread
4 garlic cloves, halved
4oz (125g) feta, thinly sliced
½lb (250g) white cheese such as Monterey Jack or Cheddar, thinly sliced

PREPARATION

1 Prepare a charcoal fire or preheat a gas grill.
2 Lightly toast the rye bread on one side over the hot fire.
3 Rub the cut cloves of garlic over both sides of the toasted bread. Place some feta on each piece of toast, then top with a few slices of Cheddar.
4 Place the toast directly on the barbecue grill, or on a baking sheet over the barbecue, and cook, preferably covered, until the cheese melts. Serve immediately.

FRUIT

Fruit is delicious on the barbecue, its natural sugars caramelizing with the heat of the flames. Because of its delicacy, fruit should be cooked over a medium to low fire, or on the cooler part of the grill top. A slice of fruit, seasoned with whatever marinade the rest of the meal is seasoned with and cooked over coals, makes a perfect accompaniment to most meat, fish, or poultry.

ROASTED BANANAS STUFFED WITH CHOCOLATE

Bananas are absolutely marvelous cooked on the barbecue, especially stuffed with chocolate! The chocolate melts as the bananas roast, and the result is an irresistibly gooey mixture. Serve with a dollop of whipped cream.

INGREDIENTS

4 medium-large ripe bananas, unpeeled
5oz (150g) milk chocolate
lightly whipped cream, if desired

PREPARATION

1 Prepare a charcoal fire or preheat a gas grill.
2 Slice through each banana lengthwise with a sharp knife, cutting through the flesh but without cutting or tearing the bottom layer of skin. Stuff each banana with about 6 squares of chocolate and then wrap in foil.
3 Place the banana parcels over medium-hot coals and leave for about 10 minutes, long enough to melt the chocolate and lightly cook the bananas. They will be soft and slightly caramelized in texture and flavor.
4 Unwrap the foil from each banana and place in bowls, skin and all. Serve immediately, with a dollop of whipped cream if desired.

VARIATION

GRILLED RUM BANANAS Peel 4 medium-large ripe but still firm bananas. Sprinkle them with 2–3 tablespoons dark rum and with brown sugar and cinnamon to taste. Cook over medium-hot coals for 2–3 minutes on each side, making sure they do not overcook and become too soft. Serve immediately, with whipped cream or ice cream.

ZESTY PINEAPPLE

This spiced fruit goes well with Eastern or Latin American flavors. Serve with Salsa (see page 124), crème fraîche, and All-American Ribs (see pages 24–25); or with Chicken Wings Satay (see page 87).

INGREDIENTS

1 ripe pineapple, peeled and cored
2–3 tbsp light brown sugar, to taste
juice of ½ lime
½–1 tbsp crushed red chili flakes, to taste

PREPARATION

1 Prepare a charcoal fire or preheat a gas grill.
2 Cut the pineapple into slices, then cut each slice into wedges. Place the pineapple in a shallow dish, add the sugar, lime juice, and red chili flakes and toss to coat well.
3 Cook over medium heat for 3–4 minutes on each side, until lightly glazed. Serve immediately.

ROASTED PEACHES WITH MASCARPONE & BASIL

INGREDIENTS

4 sweet, ripe but firm peaches, halved and pitted
2–3 tbsp butter, melted
sugar, to taste
mascarpone, to taste
handful of fresh basil leaves

PREPARATION

1 Prepare a charcoal fire or preheat a gas grill.
2 Brush the peach halves with butter and sprinkle with sugar. Cook over medium coals for 2–3 minutes on each side. Serve immediately with a few spoonfuls of mascarpone, to taste, and some basil leaves.

HONEY-BASTED FIGS WITH RASPBERRIES & ICE CREAM

Figs warmed on the grill and basted with a little honey and white wine make a sensuous and enticing dessert. The honey brings out the sweetness of the fruit, as does the heat of the grill. If ice cream is not to your taste, fresh goat cheese may be used instead.

INGREDIENTS

3–4 tbsp honey
1–2 tbsp dry white wine
12–16 ripe firm figs
1 pint (600ml) vanilla ice cream
½ pint (250g) raspberries

PREPARATION

1 Prepare a charcoal fire or preheat a gas grill.
2 Heat the honey and wine together, stirring until the honey completely dissolves into the wine. Remove from the heat.
3 Halve the figs and brush with the honey-wine mixture. If the figs are very small, use skewers or a piece of foil to prevent them from falling through the bars of the grill.
4 Place the figs over medium-low coals (this is a perfect dish for using the last of the coals after cooking dinner). Cook for only a few minutes, brushing once or twice with the basting mixture.
5 Serve the hot figs in bowls with a scoop of ice cream and some fresh raspberries.

S'MORES

For the uninitiated, S'mores are barbecued marshmallows, popped between crackers with a square of chocolate. I hadn't thought of S'mores in years until recently in the South of France: my friends had just come back from the United States with this culinary souvenir. There in Provence we ate rosemary-scented lamb and eggplants. Then out came the marshmallows. The recipe allows for 2 each, but it all depends how greedy you are.

INGREDIENTS

8 marshmallows
16 graham crackers
8 squares of chocolate

PREPARATION

1 Prepare a charcoal fire or preheat a gas grill.
2 Place the marshmallows on a stick or skewer and roast over hot coals until golden and flecked with brown. The traditional way to roast them is directly in the fire, but do not place on the cooking grill.
3 To assemble, place a hot marshmallow on a graham cracker, top with a piece of chocolate, and then another graham cracker, sandwich-style.

HOT BARBECUED ORANGES WITH FRESH STRAWBERRIES

The orange slices should just warm through and lightly caramelize. Fresh fruit adds a sweet touch — raspberries or blueberries can be used instead of strawberries.

INGREDIENTS

4 oranges, peeled and thickly sliced
4 tbsp sugar
2 tbsp Curaçao or other orange-flavored liqueur
1 pint (250g) strawberries, hulled, sliced,
and lightly sugared

PREPARATION

1 Prepare a charcoal fire or preheat a gas grill.
2 Toss the orange slices in a shallow dish with the sugar and liqueur. Let the oranges soak for about 15 minutes.
3 Place the slices over medium-hot coals for 3–4 minutes, or until the oranges are lightly cooked and the sugar has caramelized. Serve immediately, topped with the sliced strawberries.

CURAÇAO FRUIT KEBABS

Serve sizzling hot — a bowl of vanilla ice cream on the side makes a brilliant accompaniment.

INGREDIENTS

16 dried apricots (no-soak variety)
3 tbsp brandy
3 tbsp Curaçao or other orange-flavored liqueur
2 ripe nectarines or peaches, cut into bite-sized pieces
½ ripe pineapple, peeled and cut into bite-sized pieces
2 large, just ripe bananas, peeled and
cut into bite-sized pieces
2 tbsp melted unsalted butter
3–4 tbsp sugar

PREPARATION

1 Prepare a charcoal fire or preheat a gas grill. Get 8 skewers ready – wooden skewers should be soaked in cold water for 30 minutes.
2 Place the apricots in a large shallow dish. Sprinkle over half the brandy and let soak for at least 30 minutes.
3 Add the liqueur, remaining brandy, nectarines, pineapple, and bananas to the dish and mix well.
4 Thread the fruit on the skewers, reserving the marinade. Brush the skewers with melted butter and sprinkle with sugar. Cook quickly over hot coals, allowing 3–4 minutes on each side. Serve with the marinade poured over the fruit.

LUSH FRUIT FEAST

INGREDIENTS

½ ripe pineapple, peeled and sliced, then slices halved
1 crisp apple, cored and sliced
1 pear, cored and sliced
1 large ripe firm mango, peeled, pitted, and sliced
2 ripe firm apricots, pitted and halved
2 ripe firm nectarines or peaches, pitted and halved
2 ripe firm bananas, peeled and halved lengthwise
4–8 ripe figs, whole or sliced lengthwise
½lb (250g) black cherries, optional, pitted and threaded
on skewers or placed in a wire basket
sugar or honey, to taste
lemon or lime juice, to taste
white wine, rum, or liqueur, to taste
melted butter, to taste

PREPARATION

1 Prepare a charcoal fire or preheat a gas grill.
2 Macerate each variety of fruit separately in 2–4 tablespoons sugar or honey, 1 tablespoon lemon juice, and 3 tablespoons white wine, or liqueur, to taste, depending on the sweetness of the fruit.
3 Cook the fruit gently over medium coals, basting with melted butter or honey. Remove the pieces of fruit as they become warmed and lightly glazed. Serve immediately.

VARIATION

FIRE & ICE FRUIT FEAST Barbecue a few fruits and pair each with an ice cream or sorbet: for example, hot pineapple with pineapple sorbet; grilled cherries with sweet cherry ice cream; sizzling hot bananas with cinnamon-flecked banana ice cream.

SAUCES & ACCOMPANIMENTS

Barbecued foods need only the simplest of sauces to accentuate their strong flavors. Whether spicy, rich, or tangy, sauces, salsas, chutneys, and relishes will lend finesse to the final dish. Choose from rice, polenta, vegetables, and salads as accompaniments.

PESTO

INGREDIENTS

3 garlic cloves, finely chopped
3–4 cups chopped fresh basil leaves
½ cup (125ml) olive oil, or enough to make a thick paste
salt
½ cup (60g) freshly grated Parmesan, optional
3–4 tbsp chopped pine nuts or walnuts, optional

PREPARATION

1 Purée the garlic, then add the basil and work into a fine mixture. Add the olive oil and purée again until it forms a thick sauce.
2 Season with salt, add the Parmesan and nuts, if using, and process until a thick paste is formed.
3 Store in a jar with a lid, covered with a layer of oil. Pesto will keep in the refrigerator for up to 2 weeks, or in the freezer for up to 6 months.

RED CHILI AIOLI

A spicier version of the traditional Aïoli (see page 66).

INGREDIENTS

½ cup (100g) mayonnaise
1 garlic clove, finely chopped
1 tbsp mild red chili powder or pure chili powder
1 tbsp paprika
¼ tsp ground cumin
1 tbsp chopped fresh cilantro
dash of lemon or lime juice
2–3 tbsp olive oil
salt and black pepper

PREPARATION

1 Combine the mayonnaise with the garlic, chili powder, paprika, cumin, cilantro and a dash of lemon juice.
2 With a whisk or fork, slowly mix in the olive oil, a little at a time, until it is absorbed. Season to taste and chill until ready to serve.

INDONESIAN PEANUT SAUCE

This keeps for 4–5 days in the refrigerator.

INGREDIENTS

4 garlic cloves, finely chopped
2 tsp chopped fresh ginger
½ cup (150g) peanut butter
2 tbsp sugar
4 tbsp water
Tabasco, or other hot sauce, to taste
1 tbsp lemon juice
2 tbsp soy sauce
3 tbsp chopped fresh cilantro
1 tbsp sesame oil
salt and black pepper

PREPARATION

Mix the garlic with the ginger, peanut butter, and sugar. Slowly stir in the water, then, when emulsified, add the Tabasco, lemon juice, soy sauce, cilantro, and sesame oil. Season to taste.

SALSA

This keeps for up to 1 week in the refrigerator.

INGREDIENTS

3–5 garlic cloves, finely chopped
1 small onion, chopped
1 tbsp chopped fresh parsley
1 tbsp chopped fresh cilantro
10 ripe tomatoes or 13oz (400g) canned plum tomatoes, diced
1 tsp ground cumin
1–3 jalapeño or serrano chilies, finely chopped
1 tbsp lemon juice or vinegar
salt, to taste

PREPARATION

Combine the ingredients with a fork. Purée if you prefer a smooth salsa.

ROASTED GREEN CHILI SALSA

INGREDIENTS

1lb (500g) jalapeño or other medium-hot green chilies
2 tbsp olive oil
2 garlic cloves, finely chopped
salt and black pepper
juice of ½ lemon or lime

PREPARATION

1 Prepare a charcoal fire or preheat a gas grill.
2 Cook the chilies over hot coals until they are evenly charred on all sides. Remove from the barbecue and place in a paper bag for at least 2 hours to steam off the skin.
3 Peel the roasted chilies, then remove the seeds and core. Chop finely and toss with the remaining ingredients.

MOJO ROJO

INGREDIENTS

1 dried medium-hot red chili, such as cayenne or Arbol
1 tsp cumin seeds
½ cup (125ml) water
5–6 garlic cloves, finely chopped
2 tbsp paprika
½ cup (125ml) olive oil
2 tbsp red wine vinegar
salt, to taste

PREPARATION

1 Bring the chili, cumin seeds, and water to a boil and cook over a high heat for about 5 minutes.
2 Purée the garlic, add the chili mixture and paprika, then slowly blend in the olive oil. Add the vinegar and salt, and serve.

BLACK BEAN SALSA

INGREDIENTS

6oz (175g) canned black beans, drained
2–3 ripe tomatoes, diced
1 garlic clove, finely chopped
1 scallion, finely chopped
1 red or green Thai or Serrano chili, finely chopped
1 tbsp lime juice
¼ tsp ground cumin, or to taste
1–2 tbsp chopped fresh cilantro leaves
salt, to taste

PREPARATION

Toss all the ingredients together, and serve.

MOJO VERDE

INGREDIENTS

5–6 garlic cloves, finely chopped
½ green bell pepper, seeded and chopped
1 tsp cumin seeds
1 cup (30g) chopped fresh cilantro
½ cup (125ml) olive oil
2 tbsp white vinegar
salt, to taste

PREPARATION

Purée the garlic with the green pepper, cumin, and cilantro. Slowly work in the olive oil, season with vinegar and salt, and serve.

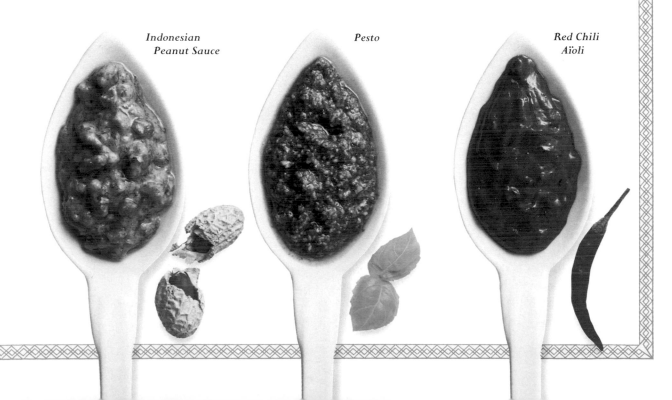

*Indonesian
Peanut Sauce*

Pesto

*Red Chili
Aïoli*

GUACAMOLE

The classic accompaniment to Fajitas (see illustration on page 26) and other Tex-Mex dishes.

INGREDIENTS

2 ripe avocados
½ onion, finely chopped
2 garlic cloves, finely chopped
2–3 tomatoes, diced
½ fresh green chili, such as jalapeño or Kenya,
finely chopped
juice of 1–2 limes
¼ tsp ground cumin
salt and ground cayenne, to taste

PREPARATION

1 Cut the avocados in half and remove the pits. Scoop out the flesh and mash coarsely.
2 Combine the avocado with the remaining ingredients. Serve immediately, or cover tightly with plastic wrap to prevent discoloration. (If the top does discolor, stir well just before serving.)

TEXAS JAILHOUSE BBQ SAUCE

I got this recipe from a dyed-in-the-wool Texan. He claimed that he had got it from his "great-grandpappy," who did a stint as a jailhouse cook.

INGREDIENTS

1 cup (300ml) ketchup
1 cup (300ml) beef stock
1 tsp mild chili powder
1 tsp paprika
1 dried chipotle chili, crumbled
½ tsp dry mustard
pinch of ground ginger
3 garlic cloves, finely chopped
2–3 tbsp dark brown sugar, or 1 tbsp molasses plus
1 tbsp brown sugar
1 tbsp Worcestershire sauce
salt and black pepper
1 tbsp lemon juice

PREPARATION

1 Combine all the ingredients in a small saucepan and bring to a boil. Reduce the heat and simmer for 10–15 minutes, or until the sauce has a smoky flavor and is well combined.
2 Allow to cool and serve at the table with barbecued steaks, chops, beef, or pork ribs. The sauce can also be brushed onto food on the grill during the last 10–15 minutes of cooking time.

WILD MUSHROOM SAUCE

INGREDIENTS

½ cup (30g) dried wild mushrooms
2 cups (500ml) hot veal or chicken stock
5 shallots, finely chopped
2 garlic cloves, finely chopped
2 tbsp butter
¼ cup (60ml) brandy
1½ cups (375g) crème fraîche
salt and black pepper
freshly ground nutmeg, to taste

PREPARATION

1 Place the dried mushrooms in a bowl and pour over the stock. Cover and leave for 30 minutes. When the mushrooms have softened, drain, squeeze dry, and dice, reserving the liquid. Strain the soaking liquid (plus the squeezed liquid).
2 Sauté the shallots and garlic in the butter until softened and lightly colored, then add the mushrooms and cook for a few minutes.
3 Pour the brandy into a long-handled ladle, then pour it into the pan, averting your face – it will spit. Boil until reduced to 2 tablespoons, then add the mushroom soaking liquid.
4 Reduce again to about ⅔ cup (175ml), then stir in the crème fraîche. Season to taste with salt, pepper, and freshly ground nutmeg.

THAI DIPPING SAUCE

INGREDIENTS

1 cup (200g) canned, chopped tomatoes,
juice included
2 tbsp dark brown sugar, or to taste
1 cup (125g) golden raisins, coarsely chopped
4 garlic cloves, finely chopped
½–1 dried red chili, crumbled
½ tsp ground cayenne, or to taste
3 tbsp cider or raspberry vinegar, or to taste
salt, to taste
3 tbsp water, plus extra if needed

PREPARATION

1 Combine the tomatoes with the sugar, raisins, garlic, chili, cayenne, vinegar, and salt. Process until it is a slightly chunky mixture, adding water as needed to give the right consistency.
2 Bring the mixture to a boil in a small saucepan and cook for a few minutes to allow the flavors to mingle. Let cool.
3 Season with extra vinegar, cayenne, salt, and sugar to taste.

SHE-DEVIL BARBECUE SAUCE

This sauce gets its kick from simmering the chipotle chili, a smoky dried chili that harbors the heat of hell. It is an ideal sauce to brush on ribs toward the end of cooking.

INGREDIENTS

1 onion, coarsely grated
3–5 garlic cloves, finely chopped
¼ cup (60ml) Worcestershire sauce
1 cup (250g) ketchup
¼ cup (60g) dark brown sugar
2–3 dried chipotle chilies
1 cup (250ml) beer, plus extra if needed
1 cup (250ml) water, plus extra if needed
1 tsp dry mustard
1 tsp mild red chili powder
1 tsp ground cumin
salt and black pepper
¼ cup (60ml) cider vinegar

PREPARATION

1 Mix together the onion, garlic, Worcestershire sauce, ketchup, dark brown sugar, chipotle chilies, beer, water, mustard, chili powder, cumin, salt and pepper, and half the vinegar.

2 Bring to a boil, then reduce the heat and simmer for 30–45 minutes, or until it forms a thick sauce. If the mixture sticks or threatens to burn, add more water or beer.

3 When the sauce is thick and flavorful, add the remaining vinegar and taste for seasoning. Remove from the heat.

4 Slather this spicy, smoky sauce on ribs or steaks when they have almost finished cooking. Serve the remainder in a bowl for guests to help themselves.

Mustard

Chili powder

Ground cumin

Salt

Black pepper

Cider vinegar

Beer

Chipotle chilies

Dark brown sugar

Worcestershire sauce

Ketchup

Garlic

Onion

RED ONION & RAISIN RELISH

This relish is an excellent accompaniment to barbecued meats (see illustration on page 97). It will keep for up to 3 days in the refrigerator.

INGREDIENTS

3 large red onions, thinly sliced
½ cup (125ml) olive oil
3–4 tbsp dark brown sugar
½ cup (90g) raisins or dried cranberries
½ cup (125ml) raspberry or cider vinegar,
or to taste
salt

PREPARATION

1 Cover the sliced onions with cold water and leave for 1 hour. Drain and dry on paper towels.
2 Heat the olive oil and sugar, stirring until the sugar dissolves. Add the onions and simmer until they go limp, 15–20 minutes.
3 Stir in the raisins and vinegar. Continue to simmer until most of the liquid has evaporated and the onions are soft and melting. Season with salt and a dash more vinegar if needed.

TOMATO & GINGER CHUTNEY

This chutney is the ideal accompaniment for barbecued fish.

INGREDIENTS

1 small onion, chopped
2 garlic cloves, coarsely chopped
1 tbsp butter
1 tsp chopped fresh ginger
pinch of ground ginger
1 green jalapeño, Kenya, or serrano chili, chopped
pinch of ground coriander
4 ripe tomatoes, diced
1–2 tsp sugar
salt, to taste
dash of vinegar, to taste

PREPARATION

1 Sauté the onion and garlic in the butter until softened, then add the ginger root, ground ginger, chili, and coriander.
2 Stir for a few minutes to blend the flavors, then add the tomatoes and sugar and cook over medium-high heat for 3–5 minutes, or until it forms a sauce.
3 Season the chutney to taste with salt and vinegar. Serve at room temperature.

BEET CHUTNEY

INGREDIENTS

4½oz (140g) pickled beets, diced
1 onion, diced
3 garlic cloves, coarsely chopped
2 tomatoes, diced
½ cup (125g) sugar
½ tsp salt
½ Scotch bonnet or other hot chili, chopped
1 tsp dried mint
¼ cup (60ml) red wine vinegar
2 tbsp currants
1 tbsp tamarind paste
½ tsp ground coriander
1 tsp curry powder
juice of ½ lemon

PREPARATION

1 Place the vegetables, sugar, salt, chili, mint, vinegar, and currants in a small saucepan.
2 Bring to a boil, then lower the heat and simmer until the liquid is nearly evaporated and the vegetables have become almost jam like.
3 Stir in the tamarind paste, coriander, curry powder, and lemon juice and remove from the heat. Serve at room temperature.

THAI GREEN MANGO RELISH

INGREDIENTS

1 green mango, slightly under ripe, peeled and diced
1 tbsp sugar, or to taste
¼ tsp salt, or to taste
½ small red Thai chili, very thinly sliced
½ small green Thai chili, very thinly sliced

PREPARATION

Toss the diced mango with the sugar, salt, and chilies. Serve with grilled fish or kebabs.

GUAVA-APPLE RELISH

INGREDIENTS

2 guavas, peeled and diced
1 small apple, peeled, cored, and diced
dash of lemon juice, to taste
pinch of sugar, to taste

PREPARATION

Combine all the ingredients and chill until ready to serve.

CUCUMBER-YOGURT RELISH

See illustration on pages 130–31.

INGREDIENTS

1 cup (250g) plain yogurt
½ cucumber, finely diced
2–3 garlic cloves, finely chopped
2 tbsp chopped fresh cilantro or parsley
2 tsp chopped fresh mint
salt, to taste
pinch of ground cayenne, optional

PREPARATION

Combine all the ingredients in a bowl and keep chilled until ready to serve. Sprinkle with a pinch of cayenne, if liked.

MIXED FRUIT CHUTNEY

See illustration on pages 130–31.

INGREDIENTS

½ cup plus 2 tbsp (150ml) cider or fruit vinegar
1 onion, chopped
2 tbsp water
1 tsp ground ginger
zest of ½ orange, chopped
½ tsp salt
pinch of ground cinnamon
1 garlic clove, finely chopped
pinch of crushed, dried, red chili peppers
½ cup (125g) light brown sugar
2 small ripe pears, peeled and diced
1 tart green apple, diced
3 tbsp golden raisins, dried cherries, or dried cranberries
2 tomatoes, diced
½ Scotch bonnet or other hot chili, chopped

PREPARATION

1 Mix together ½ cup (125ml) of the vinegar, the onion, water, ginger, orange zest, salt, cinnamon, garlic, and crushed chili peppers in a small saucepan. Bring to a boil.
2 Add the sugar, pears, apple, raisins, tomatoes, and chopped chili, then reduce the heat to a slow simmer.
3 Cook until the fruit is soft and the liquid has almost all evaporated. Adjust the sweet-sour balance, adding the remaining vinegar to taste.
4 Let cool and serve at room temperature, or pour into sterilized jars while hot and seal. The chutney will keep sealed for up to 1 year.

PINEAPPLE & RED PEPPER CHUTNEY

This relish is delicious with duck, pork, or chicken.
See illustration on pages 130–31.

INGREDIENTS

1 pineapple, about 2lb (1kg), peeled, cored, and diced
½ red pepper, cored, seeded, and diced
½ lemon, thinly sliced
½ tsp salt
1 tsp ground cinnamon
1 cup (175g) light brown sugar
1 cup (175g) granulated sugar
½ Scotch bonnet or other hot red chili, chopped
¼ tsp ground allspice
3 tbsp white vinegar or fruit vinegar
2½ tbsp currants
¼ tsp cumin seeds

PREPARATION

1 Place all the ingredients, except 1 tablespoon of vinegar, in a saucepan and bring to a boil.
2 Reduce the heat and simmer until the fruit is cooked through and the liquid nearly evaporated.
3 Adjust the sweet-sour balance, adding the remaining vinegar to taste. Let cool and serve, or pour hot into sterilized jars and seal. The chutney will keep sealed for up to 1 year.

PICKLED ONION RINGS

See illustration on page 131.

INGREDIENTS

3 large red onions, peeled and sliced crosswise
¼ cup (60ml) olive oil
6 dried bay leaves, crumbled, or ½ tsp herbes de Provence
½ tsp marjoram
pinch of ground allspice
½ cup (125ml) vinegar
1 garlic clove, finely chopped
1 tbsp dark brown sugar, or to taste
large pinch of cumin seeds
salt, to taste

PREPARATION

1 Separate the onion slices into rings and mix with the other ingredients, turning to coat well. Taste for seasoning, then leave for 1–3 hours at room temperature, or overnight in the refrigerator.
2 Serve the pickle immediately, or spoon into a sterilized jar and seal. It will keep for up to 1 year.

*Watercress, Grapefruit,
Orange, & Red Pepper
Salad
(see page 135)*

*Clockwise from top: Salsa (see page 124)
Mixed Fruit Chutney (see page 129)
Pickled Onion Rings (see page 129)
Guacamole (see page 126)
Cucumber-Yogurt Relish (see page 129)
Pineapple & Red Pepper Chutney (see page 129)*

Middle Eastern
Spiced Pilaf
(see page 133)

Mojo Rojo
(see page 125)

CAMPFIRE BEANS

If short of time, use a 13oz (400g) can of pinto beans, adding more liquid if the mixture seems too thick.

INGREDIENTS

1 cup (250g) pinto beans
1 onion, coarsely chopped
½ cup (125ml) She-Devil Barbecue Sauce (see page 127)
1 bacon slice, optional

PREPARATION

1 Cover the pinto beans with cold water and let soak overnight.
2 Drain the beans, return to the pan, and cover with fresh water. Bring to a boil, then reduce the heat and simmer for about 2 hours, or until the beans are tender.
3 Combine the beans and their cooking liquid (or the can of beans plus extra liquid) with the onion and the barbecue sauce and place in a pan that can withstand the heat of the barbecue. Top with the bacon slice, if using, then cover.
4 Bake over a cool part of the barbecue for about 1 hour, or long enough for the beans to absorb the smoky scent of the sauce. Remove the lid; if the sauce is thin, return the pan to the barbecue without a cover to let some of the liquid evaporate.

MEDITERRANEAN VEGETABLES WITH SPAGHETTINI

INGREDIENTS

1lb (500g) spaghettini
a selection of Chargrilled Vegetables, such as fennel bulb, red pepper, zucchini slices, and eggplant slices, cut into bite-sized pieces (see page 10)
3 tbsp olive oil
3 tbsp tomato purée
3 garlic cloves, finely chopped
10 sun-dried tomatoes in oil, drained and diced
handful of fresh basil leaves, coarsely chopped
freshly grated pecorino or Parmesan

PREPARATION

1 Cook the spaghettini in salted, boiling water until it is al dente, then drain.
2 Meanwhile, heat the chopped barbecued vegetables (and any juices) with the olive oil and tomato passata.
3 Toss the pasta with the vegetables, garlic, and sun-dried tomatoes.
4 Serve immediately, sprinkled with the chopped basil and cheese.

REFRIED BEANS

Refried beans, frijoles refritos, are excellent prepared from dried pinto beans, but if you are short of time, use a 13oz (400g) can of refried beans. Add enough water to give the right consistency (see below) and heat over the barbecue. The beans are a traditional accompaniment with Fajitas (see illustration on page 26).

INGREDIENTS

2 cups cooked pinto beans (see steps 1–2 left), plus about ½ cup (125ml) of the cooking liquid
¼ cup (60ml) vegetable oil
1 onion, finely chopped
salt, to taste
¼ tsp ground cumin
large pinch of mild chili powder
½lb (250g) grated cheese, such as Monterey Jack, mild Cheddar, or Pecorino

PREPARATION

1 Mash the cooked pinto beans into the cooking liquid with a potato masher, leaving about a third of the beans whole or partially whole to give a chunky-textured purée.
2 Heat the oil in a large saucepan, add the chopped onion, and sauté until softened. Add salt to taste, sprinkle with the cumin and chili powder, then add about ½ cup (125ml) of the bean mixture.
3 Cook over high heat until the mixture thickens and reduces in volume, then add more puréed beans, stirring and mashing as you cook.
4 When all the beans have been added and the mixture has formed a thick purée about the consistency of mashed potatoes, it is ready.
5 Sprinkle the bean purée with the cheese and heat until the cheese melts. (Do this on the barbecue for an extra smoky scent.)

BARBECUED VEGETABLE TORTILLA SOUP

Add extra vegetables to the barbecue while cooking, then make this soup the following day.

INGREDIENTS

1 onion, chopped
4–5 garlic cloves, finely chopped
1 tbsp olive oil
½ tsp ground cumin
½ tsp mild chili powder
½ tsp paprika
1 cup (250g) diced tomatoes, fresh or canned
1 quart (1 liter) stock
a selection of Chargrilled Vegetables (see page 10),
cut into bite-sized pieces
¼ tsp dried oregano
salt and black pepper
Tabasco, or other hot chili sauce, to taste
10oz (300g) white cheese, such as Monterey Jack
or Pecorino, sliced
1 tbsp chopped fresh cilantro
juice of 1 lime
4 big handfuls of tortilla chips

PREPARATION

1 Lightly sauté the onion and garlic in the olive oil until soft, then sprinkle in the cumin, chili powder, and paprika and cook a few minutes longer.
2 Add the tomatoes, stock, and barbecued vegetables, then bring to a boil. Reduce the heat and simmer for about 15 minutes.
3 Season with oregano, salt, pepper, and Tabasco. Then place some cheese in each bowl and ladle the hot soup over it. Sprinkle with cilantro and lime juice. Serve immediately, topped with a handful of tortilla chips.

GARLIC & SCALLION MASH

See illustration on page 93.

INGREDIENTS

3lb (1.5kg) potatoes, peeled
1 cup (250ml) milk
1½ garlic bulbs, separated into cloves but unpeeled
2–3 scallions, thinly sliced
¼lb (125g) butter, or to taste
salt and black pepper

PREPARATION

1 Cook the potatoes in boiling salted water until they are just tender, then drain.
2 Meanwhile, bring the milk to the boil with the garlic. Reduce the heat and simmer until the garlic is tender, about 20 minutes. Pass the garlic cloves through a sieve. Discard the skins.
3 Mash the potatoes with the milk and garlic. Mix in the scallions and two-thirds of the butter. Season and serve with the remaining butter on top.

ROASTED VEGETABLES VINAIGRETTE

INGREDIENTS

a selection of Chargrilled Vegetables (see page 10)
Classic Vinaigrette (see page 44)
1 garlic clove, finely chopped
2 shallots or small onions, finely chopped
1 tbsp chopped fresh herbs
salt and black pepper

PREPARATION

Dice the vegetables and toss with the vinaigrette. Add the garlic, shallots, herbs, and seasoning.

MIDDLE EASTERN SPICED PILAF

See illustration on page 131.

INGREDIENTS

¾ cup (90g) almonds, slivered or whole
4 tbsp butter
2oz (60g) spaghetti, broken up
2 onions, thinly sliced lengthwise
½ tsp ground cinnamon
¼ tsp ground cumin
1 cup (250g) long-grain rice
2 cups (500ml) hot chicken stock
¾ cup (100g) raisins

PREPARATION

1 Sauté the almonds in 1 tablespoon butter until golden brown. Remove from the pan and drain.
2 Add another tablespoon of butter and brown the spaghetti lightly. Remove from the pan and drain.
3 Sauté the onions in another tablespoon of butter until soft and golden. Sprinkle with half the cinnamon and cumin. Remove from the pan.
4 Sauté the rice in the remaining butter until golden, about 3–4 minutes. Add the hot stock, raisins, and remaining cinnamon and cumin. Cover and cook over low heat until the rice is half done.
5 Add the spaghetti to the rice, cover, and cook until the rice and spaghetti are al dente. Fork in the onions and serve topped with the almonds.

ROSEMARY POLENTA

Polenta, poured onto a flat plate or board, is cut into slabs and cooked over the open fire throughout much of the Balkans and northern Italy. Serve with sausages, poultry, or any hearty meat dish, or top with morsels of prosciutto, cheese, and herbs for a tasty snack.

INGREDIENTS

*1 cup (200g) dried polenta, or enough for 4–5 people
salt, to taste
2–3 tsp finely chopped fresh rosemary
⅓ cup (90ml) melted butter or olive oil, plus butter
to grease
freshly grated Parmesan, to taste*

PREPARATION

1 Cook the polenta in salted water according to package directions, then stir in the rosemary.
2 Meanwhile, butter a large shallow pan. Pour in the hot polenta and spread it evenly. Let cool.
3 Prepare a charcoal fire or preheat a gas grill.
4 When cool, cut the polenta into diamonds, fingers, circles, or any other shape you like.
5 Brush the polenta pieces with melted butter or olive oil, then cook over hot coals until they are slightly browned with marks from the grill. Sprinkle with Parmesan and serve immediately.

SOUTHEAST ASIAN NOODLE SALAD

See illustration on page 17.

INGREDIENTS

*½lb (250g) Chinese rice noodles
soy or fish sauce, to taste
2 tbsp vegetable oil
3 scallions, thinly sliced
½ cucumber, diced
¼ red pepper, diced
Chinese or other chili paste, to taste
juice of ½ lime
¼ cup (45g) dry-roasted peanuts*

PREPARATION

1 Cover the noodles with boiling water and let soften for about 5 minutes. Rinse in cold water.
2 Bring a pan of water to a boil and add the softened noodles. Cook until just tender, about 3 minutes. Drain and rinse in cold water.
3 Mix together the soy or fish sauce, vegetable oil, scallions, cucumber, pepper, chili paste, and lime juice. Toss with the noodles.
4 Serve the noodles sprinkled with the peanuts.

MACARONI SALAD

*Serve with a hearty meat dish, such as
All-American Ribs (see page 24).*

INGREDIENTS

*½lb (250g) small pasta, such as conchigliette or tubetti
2 celery stalks, chopped
3 scallions, thinly sliced
½ red bell pepper, cored, seeded, and diced
½ onion, chopped
1 tomato, diced
1 tbsp chopped fresh parsley
½ tsp paprika
½ cup (125g) mayonnaise
3 tbsp mild Dijon mustard
salt and black pepper*

PREPARATION

1 Cook the pasta in boiling salted water until al dente, then drain. Rinse the pasta in cold water and drain well again.
2 Toss the pasta in a bowl with the remaining ingredients. Chill until ready to serve.

CUCUMBER, CARROT, RED CABBAGE, & GREEN MANGO SALAD

*An ideal accompaniment to spicy oriental dishes,
such as Bangkok-Style Turkey (see page 87).*

INGREDIENTS

*½ cucumber, cut into julienne
1 carrot, coarsely grated
¼ head of red cabbage, thinly sliced
1 green mango, peeled, pitted, and cut into strips
2 scallions, thinly sliced
1 tbsp chopped fresh cilantro
¼–½ green Thai or other hot chili, or to taste,
finely chopped
1 tbsp soy sauce
3 tbsp rice, cider, or fruit vinegar
2 tbsp sugar, or to taste
¼ cup (45g) dry-roasted peanuts*

PREPARATION

1 Mix together the cucumber, carrot, red cabbage, mango, scallions, cilantro, and chili in a salad bowl.
2 Just before serving, mix the soy sauce with the vinegar and sugar.
3 Pour the dressing over the salad and toss well, then sprinkle with the peanuts.

WATERCRESS, GRAPEFRUIT, ORANGE, & RED PEPPER SALAD

INGREDIENTS

1 grapefruit, sliced
2 oranges, sliced
1 red pepper, cored and sliced or diced
3 cooked beets, diced, optional
1 bunch of watercress
2 tbsp olive oil
1 tbsp raspberry vinegar

PREPARATION

Arrange the fruit, pepper, beets, if using, and watercress on a platter, or toss together in a salad bowl. Sprinkle with the olive oil and vinegar and serve immediately.

A PLATE OF GREENS & HERBS

The simplest, freshest accompaniment to almost any barbecued food is a plate of crisp, fresh raw vegetables and herbs. Your choice will determine the accent of the meal. Sprinkle with Classic Vinaigrette (see page 44) if desired.

INGREDIENTS

*fresh cilantro, dill, scallions, and mint;
or fresh tarragon and curly endive leaves; or
fresh cilantro, mint, and green chilies; or
mixed green leaves, fresh basil, and rosemary; or
red peppers, thinly sliced onions, chilies, shredded
lettuce, and lemon juice; or bean sprouts,
peppers, scallions, thinly sliced celery, and
fresh cilantro; or parsley, sweet marjoram,
and a fennel bulb, thinly sliced*

*Watercress,
Grapefruit,
Orange, & Red
Pepper Salad*

MENU PLANNING

A barbecue can be a feast for a special occasion, with each course cooked on the coals – including dessert; or you may choose to barbecue just one dish while you prepare the rest indoors.

Barbecues are surprisingly adaptable, and it is easy to create outdoor menus for all sorts of events, from Sunday lunch to a children's party or an elegant dinner. They are also perfect for vegetarian meals.

RUSTIC ITALIAN DINNER

Each of these courses is redolent of memorable Italian meals. Grilled artichokes are a Sicilian delicacy, and the flavor of the lamb is enhanced by the fragrant smoke. A handful of figs roasted on the dying embers makes a wonderful dessert.

Artichokes with Tomato-Tapenade
Vinaigrette (page 56)

———

Italian Breast of Lamb (page 96)

Chargrilled Vegetables (page 10)

Rosemary Polenta (page 134) topped with a zesty
Italian tomato sauce and Parmesan cheese

———

Honey-Basted Figs with Raspberries
& Ice Cream (page 121)

ECLECTIC VEGETARIAN DINNER

There are so many vegetable dishes suitable for the barbecue that the days of planning a meal around meat or poultry are long gone. This menu is bright and healthful, with a tangy salad to balance the rich flavors.

Halloumi, Tomato, & Bay Leaf Kebabs (page 119)

Leeks with Creamy Beet Vinaigrette (page 51)

———

Stuffed Eggplant (page 56)

Watercress, Grapefruit, Orange, & Red Pepper Salad
(page 135)

Tofu Tikka in Tomato-Pea Masala (page 59)

———

Curaçao Fruit Kebabs (page 122)

Honey-Basted Figs with Raspberries & Ice Cream

Watercress, Grapefruit, Orange, & Red Pepper Salad

SUNDAY LUNCH

Sunday lunch is one of the glories of the week, when family and friends can gather for a carefree meal. In the summer, this occasion is a natural for the barbecue because both cook and guests can relax outdoors away from the heat of the kitchen. This menu is decidedly South of the Border, as Sunday lunch is a great tradition in Mexico as well.

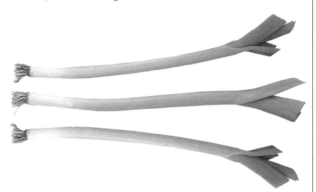

Bruschetta with Tapenade & Arugula (pages 112–13)

———•———

*Grilled scallions or leeks
(see Chargrilled Vegetables, page 10)*

Yucatecan Turkey (page 91)

Guava Apple Relish (page 128)

Black Bean Salsa (page 125) with boiled rice

———•———

Zesty Pineapple (page 120)

Yucatecan Turkey

BALKAN & MEDITERRANEAN MIDSUMMER BARBECUE

In Balkan and Mediterranean countries most cooking and eating takes place outdoors all through the summer. A rich cuisine of barbecued foods and flavors has developed, with vegetables and fish being a favorite specialty.

Mediterranean Kebabs (page 59)

———•———

Barbecued zucchini and sliced eggplant, served with olive oil, garlic, parsley, and vinegar (see Chargrilled Vegetables, page 10)

Trout Wrapped in Grape Leaves with Bean Sauce (page 61)

Bulgarian Cheese & Onion Flat Bread (page 118)

———•———

Chilled grapes and a selection of cheeses

Trout Wrapped in Grape Leaves with Bean Sauce

FLAVORS OF SOUTHEAST ASIA

Southeast Asian cuisine features food cooked over the fire: the smoky scent enhances the spicy hot seasonings to create tastes that arc invigorating in the sultry climate.

Malaysian Chili Shrimp (page 74)

———•———

Thai-Inspired Pork (page 106)

Southeast Asian Noodle Salad (page 134)

Far Eastern Broccoli (page 53)

———•———

Lush Fruit Feast (page 123)

SPICY SUN-DRENCHED SEAFOOD DINNER

Kebabs of skewered marinated fish and a platter of seafood with spicy mango relish make an enticing sun-splashed menu. Serve chocolate-stuffed bananas for a self-indulgent dessert.

Pasta tossed with Sun-Dried Tomato and Basil Butter (page 43)

Fish Kebabs (page 60)

———•———

Seafood with Mango-Pepper Relish (page 76) and a salad of al dente green beans, wedges of tomato, and Niçoise olives

———•———

Roasted Bananas Stuffed with Chocolate (page 120)

Seafood with Mango-Pepper Relish

VERY ELEGANT DINNER

This sophisticated menu is a splendid example of
how elegant and stylish barbecued food can be.
Serve each course separately and offer fresh fruit
for dessert. A rich Italian Stracchino cheese
would be a perfect accompaniment.

*Warm Mushroom Salad with
Pine Nuts and Tarragon (page 48)*

Grilled Asparagus (page 50)

Fillet of Beef (page 98)

Chargrilled Radicchio with Gorgonzola (page 49)

Garlic & Scallion Mash (page 133)

———•———

A selection of sweet fresh fruit and ripe cheeses

OPEN-AIR PARTY FROM THE FRENCH-ITALIAN BORDER

The region of France and Italy that follows the
Côte d'Azur and Nice through Monaco, Portofino,
and Genoa offers some of the most delicious food
anywhere. Fresh herbs enhance every dish,
especially lamb cooked over a barbecue.

Bruschetta with assorted toppings (pages 112–13)

———•———

Provençal Lamb (page 94)

Sausage Selection (page 111)

Grilled Eggplant Slices (page 51)

A Plate of Greens & Herbs (page 135)

Chargrilled Radicchio with Gorgonzola

Sausage Selection

MEXICAN FISH BARBECUE

The scent of fish cooked over an open fire at the beach is one of my first memories of Mexico. The spicy pastes coating the fish and seafood are particularly delicious, and the wealth of chili-based salsas enhances the meal.

Grilled Mussels with Chipotle Salsa (page 77)

———•———

Smoky-Spicy Corn Salad (page 50)

Mayan Swordfish Coated with Annatto & Chili (page 68)

Chargrilled Vegetables (page 10)

Boiled rice sprinkled with mild chili powder or ground cumin

Salsa, Roasted Green Chili Salsa, and Black Bean Salsa (pages 124–25)

Mayan Swordfish Coated with Annatto & Chili

PARTY FOR YOUNG GUESTS

Children love barbecues: there is a holiday atmosphere not found in the kitchen, and they can often prepare part of their own meal. Pizzas are perfect – let the young ones roll out the dough and choose their own toppings. To finish, S'mores are the ideal dessert for the under-12s.

Roasted Carrots (omit the ginger) (page 53)

Barbecued ears of corn (see Chargrilled Vegetables, page 10)

Barbecued Pizzas (page 114) with additional do-it-yourself toppings that children might enjoy: diced ham, bacon, lightly cooked green beans, or other vegetables

Finger salad: cucumber spears, raw broccoli, cherry tomatoes, red and yellow peppers

———•———

S'mores (page 122)

Barbecued Pizza

NORTH AFRICAN MENU

Food such as kebabs, fish, and eggplant cooked over the fire is the quintessential fare of North Africa, sold in streets and souks. Salads, too, often consist of vegetables cooked over coals, spiced with chermoula or other Moroccan dressing.

Moroccan Lamb Brochettes (in small portions) (page 98)

Mediterranean Fish (page 12)

Middle Eastern Spiced Pilaf (page 133)

Eggplant Salata (page 51)

Beets with Moroccan Dressing (page 50)

Mixed Fruit Chutney (page 129)

Middle Eastern Spiced Pilaf

CENTRAL AMERICAN FEAST

The flavors of goat cheese, chilies, and sweet onion relish make a dramatic combination for a starter. Serve the Fajitas with soft flour tortillas, so everyone can assemble their own meal.

Stuffed Peppers (page 54)

Red Onion & Raisin Relish (page 128)

Fajitas (page 99)

Guacamole (page 126)

Refried Beans (page 132)

Salsa (page 124)

Stuffed Peppers

EQUIPMENT
&
TECHNIQUES

Barbecue cooking is the essence of simplicity.
However, having the right equipment at hand helps to
make you better organized and should prevent any
last-minute dashes from kitchen to barbecue.
This section offers advice on choosing barbecues, from
simple disposable trays to covered models that can
slow-cook whole fish, poultry and large joints.
It illustrates the tools and fuels available and explains
how to get the best results from them. There is also a list
of essential ingredients for a well-stocked pantry,
and practical step-by-step instructions show how
to prepare a variety of foods for the barbecue.

BARBECUES & GRILLS

A barbecue is simply a grate or grill suspended over a bed of coals. Cooked on this primitive device, food can take on a very distinct character, absorbing the flavors and aroma of the smoke. Originally the most basic means of cooking, barbecues have become very sophisticated, and the range available runs from the disposable tray, which just needs a match to light it, to elaborate covered models capable of cooking a large roast or even a turkey. Gas and electric models are the most convenient, since they allow year-round barbecuing, give the cook absolute control, and eliminate worries about getting the charcoal alight.

COVERED KETTLES

From tiny tabletop portables to 24in (60cm) round freestanding models, these barbecues are available in a wide range of sizes. The round shape of a covered kettle barbecue reflects heat onto all surfaces and thus cooks food evenly. The cover keeps out oxygen, reducing flare-ups caused by fat falling on the fire, and also keeps the smoke inside, intensifying the smoky perfume (a kettle barbecue can also be used as a smoker). Covered kettles are very reliable, and can of course be used open as well as closed.

HOODED BARBECUES

These large, rectangular barbecues have lids and are set on rolling carts. Like kettle barbecues, they can be used covered or open. Temperature gauges, dampers to regulate the air flow, and movable grates and cooking grills give refined heat control. Extras such as rotisseries, side shelves, and warming racks are also available, making these barbecues a pleasure to cook with.

The covered kettle's rounded metal lid reflects heat all over the cooking area

Lid hooks conveniently onto side

ADVANTAGES OF COVERED KETTLES & HOODED BARBECUES
► *Enable long cooking of large cuts of meat and whole birds.*
► *Cut down on flare-ups.*
► *Give an intense smoky flavor.*

Disposable barbecues come ready to light

DISPOSABLE BARBECUES

Cheap and portable, these little pans come filled with their own charcoal and lighter fluid, ready to use. They are suitable for hamburgers, sausages, chops, or vegetables, and are excellent for picnics.

ADVANTAGES OF DISPOSABLE BARBECUES
► *Simple and inexpensive.*
► *Ideal for small spaces — even tiny balconies or patios.*

SAFETY PRECAUTIONS

♦ Never, ever squirt gasoline or any other lighter fluid directly on the fire. It can flare back in a split second and envelop you in flames. Use lighter fluid only *before* the match has been lit.

♦ Store lighter fluid in a safe place, not a warm cabinet or the trunk of a car.

♦ Keep the barbecue far from the house, dry leaves, or anything that could catch a spark and ignite. Avoid barbecuing in high winds.

♦ If barbecuing on a wooden surface such as a deck, keep the area well soaked, using a hose or bucket and water; embers can fall out of the barbecue and set the wood alight.

♦ Watch children and pets carefully to make sure they do not bump into the barbecue and turn it over.

♦ Prevent guests, especially children, from crowding around the barbecue.

♦ Do not barbecue indoors unless you have a model designed for this purpose.

♦ Keep your eye on the barbecue at all times: this is essential for safety reasons, but it can also save any food that is cooking. Sometimes just a momentary flare-up can turn dinner into something that looks more like charcoal.

♦ For the same reason, keep your tools nearby, so that you do not have to keep running back into the house to fetch them.

♦ Use long-handled cooking tools.

♦ Avoid wearing flowing sleeves when barbecuing and keep any loose clothing away from the grill.

♦ Lift a barbecue cover carefully and away from you, to avoid being burned by steam and smoke.

♦ Don't move the barbecue until the fire is out and the coals have cooled.

GAS & ELECTRIC GRILLS

Heated by gas or an electric coil, these warm up quickly (about 5–10 minutes), are easy to control and don't produce any messy ashes. Gas canisters last a long time, although in winter you should switch from butane to propane gas, which flows more quickly in cold weather. Electric models are just as convenient, though they must be sited near a power outlet. Regulating the heat on both models is easy, giving control over the cooking process.

Where year-round barbecuing is part of the culture, as in California, many houses have a barbecue as part of the kitchen equipment. Many of these barbecues use lava rock above the burner. When the cooking juices drip on to the rock it creates an aromatic smoke that flavours the food. Lava rocks are natural heat conductors. If they become too greasy, wash or burn the grease off (see unit instructions).

Basket to hold scented woods or herbs to flavor the smoke.

The heat on a gas barbecue is easy to adjust

CHARCOAL BARBECUES

Open-top barbecues can be small tabletop models or larger freestanding ones. They are ideal for quick-cooking small items such as sausages or burgers, but for large cuts of meat or whole fish you really need a lid. It is possible to improvise a lid using foil, but a covered kettle barbecue is the ideal solution. Fatty foods can cause flare-ups, so keep a spray bottle of water at hand.

HOW TO USE A BARBECUE

Cooking on a barbecue is very straightforward. No matter how sophisticated the model is, barbecuing is no more than cooking over an open fire. The most important factors are the preparation, lighting, and maintenance of the fire (see below). It is a good idea to have the food prepared in advance so that once the coals are at the right stage you will be ready to start cooking.

—————————— • ——————————

PREPARING THE FIRE

Allow about an hour to prepare the fire before you begin cooking; coals need about 45 minutes to heat up. If you underestimate how long it takes to get the coals ready, you end up with the frustrating situation of a group of eager guests gathered hopefully around the barbecue while you fumble with matches and uncooperative coals, mentally working out how quickly the food can be cooked.

For food that requires 45–60 minutes' cooking, make a bed of coals two layers deep. When cooking for longer than 45 minutes, you should add more charcoal, allowing 15 minutes for it to ignite.

LIGHTING THE FIRE

There are a number of ways to ignite a fire.
KINDLING Newspapers make the best kindling. Roll up a sheet tightly into a tube, then twist it to make a stick. Place several of these in the bottom of the fuel grate, then set evenly shaped chunks of wood, dry twigs, or sticks on top. Over this arrange coals in a pyramid so that there is some air between them. Light the newspaper and, as the fire grows, add more coals. When the coals are hot, spread them out to make an even bed.
FIRELIGHTERS These are very simple to use: just stack the coals around the firelighters, then light.
LIGHTER FLUID The most commonly used starter, this leaves a chemical taste on coals unless you let it burn off. It is dangerous if used incorrectly. Never squirt lighter fluid onto a burning fire. The flames can travel back in a split second and turn you into a human torch. Do not squirt lighter fluid onto hot coals. Immediately after you have lit the coals, put away the lighter fluid.
ELECTRIC STARTER This is an oval-shaped heating element attached to a long handle with a cord. Place the unit in the coals and plug into an electrical outlet. The starter turns red hot and sets fire to the surrounding coals. Other coals catch, quickly giving an excellent fire. The drawback is that you need a power source nearby.

FIRE CHIMNEY A perforated metal chimney with a handle, this is easy to use. Remove the cooking grill and place the chimney in the grate. Lay crumpled newspaper in the bottom, then stack coals on top and light the paper. Chimneys usually hold 45–50 coals, which light quickly. When well lit, carefully empty the coals into the grate.

TEMPERATURE REQUIRED

Most coals take about 45 minutes to burn down to the even heat required for cooking. If flames are still licking around the coals, the fire is not yet ready for cooking.
The stages of coals described in the recipes are:
HOT Red and glowing, with occasional flare-ups; the coals will begin to form a light layer of gray ash. You can hold your hand no closer than 6in (15cm) from the coals for 2–3 seconds. Lean foods that cook quickly, such as chicken breasts or fish fillets, may be placed on the grill at this stage; food to be seared can be placed over hot coals, then moved to a cooler spot on the barbecue to cook through.
MEDIUM-HOT The layer of gray ash is thicker, with a red glow only occasionally visible. You can hold your hand over the cooking grill for about 5 seconds. Suitable for ribs and chicken legs.
COOL The coals have a thick layer of gray ash, virtually no red shows, and the fire will be slower. You should be able to hold your hand over the fire for 7–8 seconds when cooking at this heat, which is suitable for long-cooking foods such as sheets of ribs and other large cuts of meat, or whole chickens or other poultry.

KEEPING THE FIRE GOING

Most charcoal burns for 45–60 minutes. For longer cooking times, you need to add more coals. Add a few coals directly to the fire or, for a large fire, heat the new supply of coals separately. A second barbecue is useful for this. Use tongs to transfer the coals.

STOKING THE FIRE

Tapping coals with tongs will knock off a little ash and heat up the fire. If the grill has vents or a hood, open them to allow air to whip up the fire. Add new coals before you begin cooking, or keep the food to one side and add coals to the other.

COOLING THE FIRE

Spread out the coals with tongs for a less intense bed of heat. Alternatively, cover the barbecue, if it has a hood, and close any vents by about half.

SHUTTING DOWN THE BARBECUE

After retrieving the last morsel from the grill, start putting the fire out. If you have cooked on an open fire, spray the coals with water. If the barbecue has a lid, cover the cooking top and close all the vents to shut off the air flow.

Don't throw away unburned material. You can reuse hardwood charcoal, if thoroughly dried after spraying. Combine old coals with fresh ones, as used material takes longer to light and does not burn as hot as fresh coals.

COOKING ON A BARBECUE

OPEN OR COVERED? When you barbecue with an open cooking top, the coals burn hotter because there is a draft. This method is excellent for small items such as chops or burgers because the higher heat chars the food quickly, sealing in the juices.

Larger items such as slabs of ribs and chicken quarters benefit from a cover. This reduces the flare-ups that could char the outside, leaving the inside raw and uncooked. Air circulates inside a covered barbecue, cooking the food evenly, much like an oven.

DIRECT COOKING Arrange the food on the grill directly over the heat of the coals. The barbecue can be either left open or covered, depending on the size, thickness, and fattiness of the food to be cooked.

INDIRECT (USING A DRIP PAN) This method is best for larger, longer-cooking items. Arrange the hot coals at the sides of the fuel bed, then place a drip pan in the center. Place the cooking grill over it and set the food on top. Cover, and let the juices drip into the pan to make a sauce. Add water, stock, or wine to the drip pan for extra moisture while cooking and for a lighter sauce. Top off every 30 minutes or as required. Skim off the fat before serving.

SEARING This is a good technique for foods that cook quickly and tend to dry out; it seals in the juices. Oil the grill and place the food over a hot fire with the cover off. Cook for 1–2 minutes on each side. Finish cooking over a cooler part of the barbecue, or take the food off the grill and let the coals burn down a little before finishing cooking.

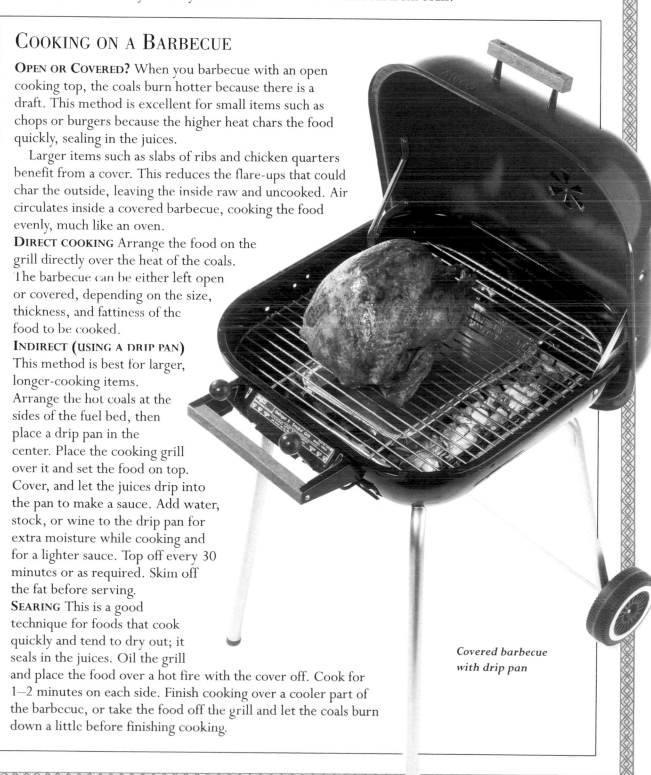

Covered barbecue with drip pan

TOOLS & MATERIALS

As with so many endeavors, having the right tools for the job makes all the difference when barbecuing. Some items, such as forks, tongs, and wire baskets, are invaluable for taking food on and off the grill quickly and for turning fragile items without breaking or dropping them. Other tools facilitate basting and glazing.

WIRE BRUSHES
The cooking grill should always be scraped clean with a wire brush after use. Oil the grill before cooking to keep food from sticking to it.

BASTING BRUSHES
Choose a long-handled brush for applying sauces and glazes. You can also make herb and vegetable brushes (see page 152).

SKEWERS
These can be made of wood, bamboo, or metal. Soak wooden or bamboo skewers in cold water for about 30 minutes before using to help prevent burning. It is best to use metal skewers for foods that need longer cooking.

MEAT THERMOMETER
Invaluable for testing if large roasts are done.

TONGS
Long-handled tongs enable you to move coals and turn food as it cooks.

HINGED BASKET
This implement holds food between two wire racks and keeps it from slipping into the fire or sticking to the grill. It is very useful for cooking and turning fish and other delicate items or small vegetables.

FORKS
Use a long-handled, double-pronged fork for placing food on the grill or for testing whether vegetables are tender.

SPATULAS
A spatula with a long handle makes it easy to turn delicate foods that fall apart if not handled with care.

FUELS

The basic fuels are briquettes, charcoal, and wood chips. Many charcoals such as mesquite and hickory add their own distinctive flavor and scent, and each variety burns at a different speed and heat. Nuts, herbs, spices, seaweed, and aromatic woods all make marvelous additions to the smoky scent of the fire, even on gas barbecues. In fact, gas barbecues often have a special compartment designed to hold scented woods or herbs.

BRIQUETTES
Containing wood scraps, sawdust, coal, and sand, these are bound with a petroleum-based substance.

MESQUITE CHARCOAL
Made by the Yaqui Indians in Mexico, this has a woody scent and is clean-burning.

LUMP CHARCOAL
This is made from whole pieces of wood, with no fillers. It burns hotter and cleaner than briquettes.

WOOD
Wood burns more quickly than charcoal. Use chunks of oak, cherry, hickory, or maple. Burn until red-hot and lightly covered with gray ash.

TO SCENT THE SMOKE
Wood chips, twigs from fruit trees, vine cuttings, fresh or dried herbs, spices, nuts, and seaweed all impart flavor and aroma.

NUTS
Lightly crack almonds, pecans, walnuts, etc., soak for 20 minutes, then toss on the fire.

FRESH OR DRIED HERBS
Place bay leaves or sprigs of thyme, lavender, rosemary, or sage on the coals or grill. Fennel is classic with fish.

SEAWEED & KELP
To impart the tang of the sea when cooking seafood or fish, add seaweed and kelp to the fire. Store dried, then soak before using.

TWIGS & WOOD CHIPS
Fruit-tree and grape-vine cuttings and wood chips can add aroma to the fire. Soak the chips for 30 minutes first.

FIREPROOF MITT
Keep several nearby for handling hoods, cooking grills, skewers, spits, drip pans, and other hot items.

SPRAY BOTTLE
Filled with water, this should be kept on hand in case of flare-ups.

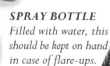

THE PANTRY

From soy sauce to chilies, peanut butter to sun-dried tomatoes, pantry contents now reflect the global table, so having a good choice on hand will give your barbecues variety and zest. Grow your own herbs, if possible, and buy others as needed. Dried herbs and spices are also essential for adding fragrance and character.

FRESH HERBS

I always try to keep a supply of fresh herbs to add their distinctive scents to marinades, flavored butters, and sauces. Basil, coriander, rosemary, thyme, oregano, marjoram, tarragon, and mint are all invaluable. Pesto made with fresh basil (see page 124) is excellent in marinades or with simple grilled dishes. Many herbs can be bought growing in pots. Keep them on a windowsill, if possible, and cut as needed. Fresh herbs can also be stored in sealed bags in the refrigerator.

Bay leaves and rosemary twigs can be used to perfume the fire. Place them on the grill or the coals to scent the smoke.

DRIED HERBS

A good supply of dried herbs is extremely useful, especially in the winter when fresh herbs are less readily available. Buy dried herbs in small quantities, store in a cool dark place, and check them regularly, as they will eventually lose their savor.

FRESH FLAVORINGS

Garlic

No other aromatic seasoning goes so well with grilled food. Studded into meats, rubbed on fish, pounded into butters, stirred into marinades, garlic enhances almost anything.

Ginger

This fresh rhizome is available in most supermarkets and should be kept in plastic wrap in the refrigerator. It can be peeled and chopped, or it can be grated, in which case it is rarely necessary to peel it first, since the skin usually catches in the grater.

Galangal

Galangal is a fresh rhizome, similar to ginger. It has an intense spicy flavor and is an important ingredient in Southeast Asian cooking. Store and prepare as for ginger.

Lemongrass

Resembling a large scallion, but smelling and tasting like essence of lemon, lemongrass is increasingly available. Peel off the outer leaves and chop the tender center stem.

The Onion Family

Finely chopped onions, shallots, and scallions give a subtle flavor to marinades, sauces, savory butters, and relishes.

Lemons, Oranges, Limes

Citrus fruit of all kinds make a fragrant addition to marinades. They can also be squeezed over cooked food and added to salsas and relishes.

DRIED SPICES & FLAVORINGS

Cumin seeds and powder, cardamom pods, coriander seeds, turmeric, chili powder and flakes, cayenne, ground ginger, garam masala, paprika, ground cinnamon and cinnamon sticks, peppercorns, star anise, and cloves are all essential for rubs and marinades. For spicy marinades and sauces, I suggest using chili powder or a mixture of chili powder and paprika if the chili is too hot. Always use freshly ground black pepper in recipes.

Other useful flavorings are dried garlic and onion powders, especially in dry rubs where

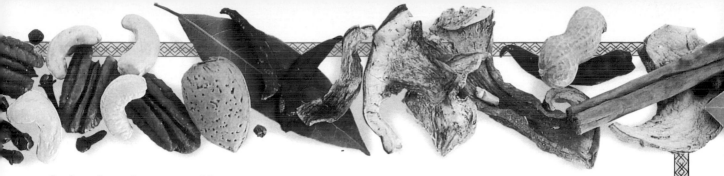

fresh garlic and onion would not combine well with the other dry ingredients.

Annatto Seeds
Available in Southeast Asian stores, these seeds give a spicy flavor and red color to food. To soften them, cover with water and boil for 5–10 minutes, then leave overnight. The next day cook for 30–45 minutes, until just tender, then puree.

Chipotle Chilies
These extremely hot, dried, smoked chilies have a unique flavor and scent. They add a great smoky flavor – and heat – to barbecue sauce.

Dried Mushrooms
Dried mushrooms such as shiitake, morels, porcini, and cepes have a foresty scent that is perfect with barbecued food. Soak in warm water for 30 minutes, then drain and squeeze dry, saving the liquid for sauces.

BOTTLED & PRESERVED FOODS

Creamed Coconut
Dissolved in water creamed coconut gives a smooth texture to spicy sauces and can be used to add a Southeast Asian flavor. Use unsweetened canned coconut milk as a substitute.

Olive Pastes
Both green and black olive pastes (tapenades) bring the scent of the Mediterranean to marinades. They are good spread over simply cooked beef, lamb, or fish steaks.

Tamarind Paste
Made from fruit pulp, this acidic flavoring is sold as a paste or in a concentrated block. Tamarind block should be soaked in hot water for 10 minutes, then squeezed out and strained.

Sun-Dried Tomatoes
These are available dry in packages, or bottled in oil. Tomatoes in oil are the most practical for barbecuing. If you buy a package of dried tomatoes, steep them in boiling water until tender, then drain and marinate in olive oil with garlic, vinegar, thyme, or herbes de Provence.

Capers
These salty, tangy flower buds add zest to poultry and fish dishes. Scatter a spoonful over turkey cutlets, or add to a brown butter sauce for sole or other fish.

Syrups
Rich maple syrup and vibrant pomegranate syrup (grenadine) add depth to both sweet and savory sauces and marinades.

NUTS & DRIED FRUIT

Nuts
The earthy crunch of all kinds of nuts – pine nuts, pistachios, pecans, almonds, cashews, and walnuts – is excellent with grilled food. Nuts can be chopped and stirred into marinades or toasted and used for cooked dishes.

Peanuts
Pureed peanuts or peanut butter add richness to Chinese marinades and form the basis of Indonesian Peanut Sauce (see page 122).

Dried Fruit
Raisins, dried apricots, and cranberries give a superbly fruity flavor to sweet and savory relishes and sauces.

OILS, CONDIMENTS, & WINES

Oils
Extra-virgin olive oil has the best flavor and aroma; make sure you choose a good-quality one, preferably cold pressed. Hazelnut, walnut, and sesame oils give a nutty flavor to marinades and sauces.

Hoisin Sauce
A red sweet-and-spicy puree based on soy beans, this is often used in Chinese-style marinades.

Mustard
Mustard adds punch to sauces, marinades, and butters. Keep whole-grain, tarragon, Dijon, and herbes de Provence mustards.

Coarse Sea Salt
Best for texture and flavor.

Soy Sauce
Use dark for "bigger" flavors; light for light meats and fish.

Vinegars
The essential vinegars are fruit vinegars, such as raspberry; wine, cider, and balsamic vinegar; and rice vinegar. Flavored vinegars are also good (see pages 44–45).

Wines
Red and white wine, sherry, port, and rice wine tenderize food and flavor marinades and sauces.

PREPARING VEGETABLES

Most vegetables can be barbecued whole or cut into chunks for kebabs. Some, like the eggplant, sweet potato, squash, and pumpkin, are excellent slow-cooked, their tender flesh scooped out and mashed for sauces, dips, or soups. Many vegetables benefit from a light marinade; others, such as artichokes and potatoes, are best parboiled. Extra onions, leeks, garlic, and tomatoes cooked on the grill make tasty ingredients for the following night's supper.

ROASTED GARLIC PUREE

Garlic purée can be added to marinades, flavored butters, aïoli, and soups. Its complex, deep yet mild garlic flavor is magnificent combined with the strong taste and smell of fresh raw garlic. Roasted garlic purée can be kept for up to a week in the refrigerator.

1 Place whole heads of garlic on the barbecue grill, letting them cook over a slow part of the fire until the flesh is soft and creamy. Separate the cloves.

2 Using a knife, squeeze or scrape out the flesh of the individual cloves. Chop or pound the flesh into a purée, or process in a food processor.

ARTICHOKES

Artichokes must be parboiled before they go on the barbecue. Trim the artichokes, then blanch them in boiling water for 15 minutes. Drain upside down, then cut in half lengthwise and scrape out the inedible "choke" with a teaspoon.

1 Trim the stem and remove the tough lower leaves. Slice off the top and trim the sharp edges of the leaves.

2 Blanch the artichokes, drain, and cut in half. Scrape out the hairy "choke" with a small spoon.

BASTING BRUSHES

Celery sticks and leeks, cut into brushes, make excellent mops for basting, as well as adding aroma. Bunches of herbs work well too, tied firmly together.

LEEK BRUSH

Trim the green ends, then slice finely through half its length with a sharp knife.

HERB BRUSH

Tie sprigs of herbs firmly together, then wind string around to make a "handle" and tie securely. Trim the ends.

CHILIES

VARIETIES There are literally hundreds of varieties of chili – those shown below are some of the most common. Fresh chilies run the gamut from mildly spicy to so hot you want to scream, if only you could find your voice. Generally, the smaller the chili, the hotter the flavor. Contrary to what many people believe, red chilies are not necessarily hotter than green ones. To prepare, chop or slice thinly. The heat is in the seeds and white pith, so remove these if preferred. Be very careful when handling chilies: always wash your hands afterward, and never touch your face.

TO BARBECUE Chilies of all sizes are a treat tossed on the barbecue, charred, then peeled. Simply place on the grill and cover to enhance the smoky scent, turning every so often. When evenly but lightly charred, remove and place in a paper bag or a bowl with a tight-fitting lid. Seal and leave for 30 minutes to steam the skins off. They should then peel easily.

Jalapeño or Fresno
Hot green or red Mexican chili, widely used.

Caribe
Sweet, mild, yellowy-green American chili.

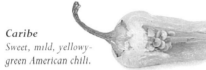

Scotch bonnet or Habañero
Very hot, red, yellow, or orange chili.

Thai
Hot red or green chili.

Birdseye
Tiny, very hot, green or red Asian chili.

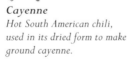

Cayenne
Hot South American chili, used in its dried form to make ground cayenne.

Poblano
Mild, dark-green Mexican chili, known as Ancho in its dried form.

Chipotle
Smoked, dried form of the jalapeño chili.

Fire candle (cayenne type)
Medium-hot, red and green chili.

Anaheim
Mild, sweet chili used for grilling and stuffing.

PREPARING SHELLFISH

Shellfish needs only simple preparation, followed by rapid cooking so it doesn't dry out and become tasteless. Make sure the pieces are not so small that they fall through the grill, or use a wire basket to hold them. Squid should be cleaned and then cooked very briefly on the grill before being cut into rings. Lobster and crab can be barbecued after cooking, absorbing the smoky flavors superbly.

CLEANING SQUID

1 *Hold the squid in one hand and pull the head and tentacles sharply away from the body, drawing out the entrails.*

2 *Cut off the head just above the tentacles. Discard the head and entrails, but reserve the tentacles.*

3 *Rinse out the squid body and remove the long, transparent beak and any remaining innards. Peel off the thin gray-pink skin and rinse again.*

PREPARING LOBSTER

Lobsters are often sold precooked and need only to be split and cleaned before barbecuing over hot coals.

2 *Pull out the round, white gravel sac near the head and pick out the long, thin intestinal vein with a knife. Discard both.*

1 *Using a heavy sharp knife, cut lengthwise down the center, through the head, body, and tail.*

WRAPPING FISH IN LEAVES

Most fish are delicious when cooked wrapped in leaves (see pages 61 and 67). Fig leaves, grape leaves, citrus leaves, and banana leaves all keep food moist and impart their own scents. Grape leaves in brine should be rinsed before use. Banana leaves are available frozen from Chinese and Asian groceries. Defrost, then cut to the size desired. Heat quickly over the barbecue to make them pliable before wrapping. Secure the bundle with fine string, toothpicks, or bamboo skewers.

Aluminum foil can be used if leaves are not available, but it does not let in the good smoky fragrance.

PREPARING MEAT

Steaks and other small cuts of meat should be of uniform thickness so that they cook evenly and no part becomes dry and listless while the rest is still rare. Splitting, pounding, and boning are all techniques that help produce an even thickness. Larger cuts of meat, whole poultry, and whole large fish, such as salmon, should be cooked slowly, covered, over indirect heat to retain their juices.

SPLITTING A CHICKEN FOR GRILLING

1 Using kitchen scissors, cut through the back of the chicken along both sides of the backbone. Discard the bone.

2 Lay the chicken on a surface, skin side up, and press down firmly with the heel of your hand to flatten it out.

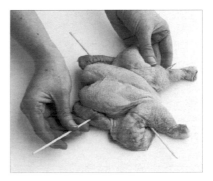

3 Thread several bamboo skewers to crisscross through the flesh and hold the chicken flat while it cooks.

POUNDING CHOPS

Pound chops between waxed paper or plastic wrap with a wooden mallet. The bones stay attached, forming a handle, while the meat cooks quickly.

BONING A TURKEY THIGH

A boned turkey thigh yields a large "steak" of tender dark meat, perfect for kebabs or for slicing.

1 Remove the skin and discard. Using a sharp knife, cut along the muscles that cover the bone. Cut the meat free, scraping to loosen the flesh.

2 Remove the bone and save for making soup. The turkey thigh can be sliced into steaks, medallions, or chunks for barbecuing.

BRINING

Brining produces moist, succulent beef or pork with a silky texture.

INGREDIENTS

*½ cup (125g) sugar
4 tbsp coarse sea salt
10 each of coriander seeds, juniper berries, and black peppercorns
5 bay leaves
1 sprig thyme
5 quarts (5 liters) water*

PREPARATION

1 Heat all the ingredients until the sugar and salt dissolve. Cool, then pour over the food to be brined.
2 Leave for 3 days, then rinse the food well and dry. Rub with olive oil before placing on the barbecue.

NUTRITIONAL INFORMATION

RECIPE	KCAL	PRO	FAT(S)	FAT(U)	CARB	SOD.	RECIPE	KCAL	PRO	FAT(S)	FAT(U)	CARB	SOD
A Plate of Greens & Herbs	117	2.1	1.4	8.0	6.2	143	Down-Home Texas BBQ Chicken	498	51.5	3.3	8.8	45.3	2686
All-American Ribs	1055	45.4	30.6	61.8	8.4	853	Duck with Thyme, Lavender, etc.	832	97.9	12.9	27	14.8	942
Anticuchos	444	57.4	6.4	13.0	5.9	611	Eggplant Salata	109	4	1.5	7.2	4	305
Artichokes with Vinaigrette	595	1.9	9.3	53.7	5.6	474	Eggplant & Corn Soup	148	4.1	1.4	7.6	13.6	596
Asparagus Pizza	816	41.8	15.1	16.8	97.7	1979	Fajitas	488	38.4	5.9	8.6	175	437
Azerbaijani-Style Kebabs	307	29.1	8.8	6.8	5.6	695	Far Eastern Broccoli	83	8.9	0.6	1.4	7.9	677
Bangkok-Style Turkey	530	76	2.7	4.8	41.8	666	Fillet of Beef	694	74.8	10.5	29.1	1.9	462
Barbecued Hoisin Lamb	726	37.5	24.3	31.5	19.4	747	Fire-Baked Potatoes	149	3.2	0.3	2.4	29.8	12
Barbecued Lamb Noisettes	898	30.7	46.8	35.1	7.5	715	Fire-Cooked Shallots	169	2.3	1.7	9.9	14.8	297
Barbecued Veal Chops	1062	62.9	44.9	38.5	7.4	600	Fire-Roasted Cherry Tomatoes	80	0.7	1.2	6.5	2.1	298
Barbecued Vegetable Tortilla Soup	607	35	19.3	24.4	20.6	1549	Fire-Roasted Rabbit	909	95.7	19.0	39.2	0.9	4621
Basque Chicken	738	37.6	11.8	43.7	3.7	706	Fish Kebabs	326	29.0	3.3	16.4	8.5	796
Beet Chutney	154	1.4	-	0.3	38.8	340	Garlic & Scallion Mash	560	10.3	23.1	5.4	70.0	588
Beet with Moroccan Dressing	158	2.1	1.9	10.8	9.6	442	Georgian Shish Kebab	687	55.8	8.6	34.3	9.9	117
Black Bean Salsa	50	4.2	0.1	0.4	7.4	325	Greek Pork Chops	802	72.5	13.9	41.7	3.3	524
Brine-Cured Pork Roast	1503	113.0	37.1	59	44.4	1149	Green Beans with Garlic Butter	143	2.8	8.9	4.0	4.5	408
Bruschetta	244	7.8	0.8	4.7	41.6	553	Grilled Asparagus	340	6.5	4.9	28.1	3.4	508
Bruschetta & Sun-dried Tomatoes	417	16.2	9.1	11.0	45.9	672	Grilled Eggplant Slices	40	1.6	0.3	1.5	4.2	392
Burgers	854	50.4	19.3	39.1	34.3	1656	Grilled Game Hens	346	39.1	11.3	9.5	0.9	531
Butterflied Leg of Lamb	1101	94.3	35.9	41.0	2.0	514	Grilled Mussels with Salsa	297	55.0	1.9	4.7	4.5	956
Cajun Spiced Fish	180	33.4	2.6	1.9	1.3	173	Grilled Salmon with Leeks	579	42.7	14.9	28.1	5.1	1018
Campfire Beans	264	9.2	1.6	3.0	45.4	1266	Guacamole	160	2.2	3.3	11.6	4.5	203
Caribbean Spicy Chicken Wings	258	32.7	2.7	8.3	7.85	115	Guava-Apple Relish	15	0.1	-	-	3.8	1
Char Siu-Style Pork	535	63.1	9.3	15.7	12.1	757	Haddock with Creole Remoulade	384	32.6	7.7	19.8	0.7	794
Chargrilled Radicchio	446	9	12	30.8	6.6	787	Halloumi Kebabs	276	10.6	10.9	13.2	4.3	908
Chargrilled Scallions	180	1.9	2.3	13.5	8.1	516	Herb-Cured Barbecued Salmon	403	34.8	9.1	19.6	1.5	630
Chargrilled Vegetables	580	10	7	40	33	572	Honey-Basted Figs	140	3.4	0.3	0.5	31.3	9
Chicken Breasts with Mushrooms	961	64.1	40.2	30.9	8.3	873	Hot Barbecued Oranges	193	3.0	-	0.3	43.4	15
Chicken Breasts with Pesto	836	67.9	12.5	49.1	1.6	616	Indonesian Game Hens	472	48	4.9	16.2	24.4	1567
Chicken Tikka	455	68.7	8.3	9.4	5.5	596	Indonesian Peanut Sauce	300	10.5	4.5	19.2	12.3	860
Chicken Wings Satay	725	45.2	8.1	30.0	49.1	2753	Italian Breast of Lamb	615	56.2	19.7	22.4	3.0	409
Chicken with Chives & Tarragon	428	59.7	4.5	15.8	0.1	452	Jerk Pork Ribs	952	56.6	22.3	48.2	15.4	514
Chicken with Garlic & Lime	560	49.0	8.9	27.9	6.6	576	Korean Beef or Lamb	824	75.7	17.1	33.8	12.6	1931
Chicken with Mustard & Garlic	443	50.0	5.0	19.1	7.3	443	Leeks with Beet Vinaigrette	346	3.8	11	21.2	11.2	437
Chicken with Watercress Sauce	515	52.2	13.1	17.4	9.0	738	Lobster with Cilantro Butter	405	15.3	26.0	10.9	3.3	815
Chili-Cheese Turkey Breasts	337	46.1	7.4	8.7	2.1	747	Loin Chops with Green Masala	971	39.8	32.8	56.1	3.3	613
Chili-Citrus Shrimp Skewers	613	45.1	12.4	27.9	11.2	3735	Lush Fruit Feast	246	4.1	2.5	1.3	51.3	36
Chili-Citrus Squid	232	20.4	1.9	10.6	8.7	515	Macaroni Salad	312	4.0	3.8	21.4	18.6	677
Cod with Sun-Dried Tomato Relish	313	35.4	2.4	14.8	4.8	488	Malaysian Chili Shrimp	370	44.6	2.3	11.5	18.6	3864
Crisp-Crusted Flat Breads	497	12.4	1.1	8.1	97.2	490	Mango-Mustard Glazed Duck	784	95.5	10.7	27.6	14.8	2132
Cucumber, Carrot, etc, Salad	122	4.0	1.1	4.7	14.0	343	Maple-Roasted Sweet Potatoes	395	4.2	13	5.6	56	245
Cucumber-Yogurt Relish	59	4.2	1.2	0.8	6.2	246	Mayan Swordfish	282	55.6	2.3	7.0	4.7	999
Cumin Roast Lamb	783	41.6	28.4	31.1	20.8	615	Meat Patties Stuffed with Feta	956	36.3	20.9	64.4	12.0	2248
Curaçao Fruit Kebabs	379	6.8	4.8	2.0	66.7	56	Mediterranean Fish	443	4.8	5.8	24.2	0.7	606
Curried Cod with Lime	432	33.9	21.8	9.1	2.7	1001	Mediterranean Kebabs	279	41.0	3.6	20.1	12.5	411
Double Garlic Pizza	889	38.0	12.7	23.6	109.4	1418	Mediterranean Pizza	837	38.7	17.9	16.7	98.6	2288

RECIPE	KCAL	PRO	FAT(s)	FAT(u)	CARB	SOD	RECIPE	KCAL	PRO	FAT(s)	FAT(u)	CARB	SOD
Mediterranean Vegetables	471	10.2	5.3	25.6	40.8	213	Southeast Asian Noodle Salad	195	5.4	2.0	11.5	13.7	603
Middle Eastern Spiced Pilaf	441	8.6	10.0	16.0	46.0	262	Spicy Seafood Soup	252	33.2	1.7	8.5	6.3	1906
Mixed Fruit Chutney	213	1.7	-	0.3	53.9	310	Spiedini	610	22.7	14.5	32.0	26.8	785
Mojo Rojo	290	0.7	4.6	26.7	1.3	197	Steak & Mushrooms	848	60.0	36.9	24.7	3.3	744
Mojo Verde	289	0.6	4.6	26.7	1.3	197	Steak alla Mexicana	617	90.1	9.1	15.3	10.0	1234
Monkfish Kebabs with Aioli	893	37.2	13.7	68.6	0.8	708	Steak Jalisco Style	713	71.1	15.5	26.7	10.4	634
Moroccan Lamb Brochettes	885	45.0	32.2	47.8	3.3	525	Stuffed Eggplant	637	19.7	18.4	41.9	4.1	666
Mussel Brochettes	815	38.3	19.6	36.5	12.2	2800	Stuffed Peppers	289	9.5	9.5	16.8	4.1	605
Mustard-Flavored Mackerel	328	20.2	5.1	28.4	1.6	694	Swordfish Steaks Capri	500	45.6	5.2	28.6	3.8	650
New Potatoes & Yams	475	4.8	5.0	28.4	41.3	510	Szechuan Chicken	538	45.4	5.4	26.7	15.6	1427
Oysters with Spinach Relish	148	13.6	6.9	3.5	0.2	1292	Texas Jailhouse BBQ Sauce	150	2.9	-	0.8	35.8	1264
Paillards of Chicken	457	41.0	7.4	24.3	2.4	457	Thai Dipping Sauce	133	2.0	-	0.3	32.3	207
Pesto	442	8.0	8.5	36.6	1.1	164	Thai Green Mango Relish	26	0.3	-	0.1	6.3	195
Pickled Onion Rings	184	1.3	2.2	13.0	11.2	204	Thai-Inspired Pork	627	64	7.7	21.1	17.3	991
Pineapple & Red Pepper Chutney	489	1.8	-	0.7	127	304	Thai-Style Shrimp	156	16.9	5.3	2.9	3.7	1454
Pizza Dough	412	12.1	0.5	2.4	89.8	976	Thanksgiving Turkey	592	101	8.9	8.4	3.1	423
Pizzette with Field Mushrooms	701	35.3	12.9	10.8	92.3	1559	Tofu Tikka in Tomato-Pea Masala	226	12.2	9.3	4.8	13.1	730
Pomegranate-Cranberry Duck	838	97.4	10.7	26.1	21.4	1149	Tomato & Ginger Chutney	62	1.2	2.2	1.2	6.8	36
Pork & Gingered Fruit	792	53.4	20.7	27.0	38.8	555	Topinka	587	30.6	197	10.1	52.9	1521
Pounded Veal	741	60.5	28.4	26.6	1.0	3212	Tostadas Ibiza	491	20.1	12.3	22.5	26.1	997
Provençal Fish in Grape Leaves	227	33.5	1.4	7.5	3.3	437	Trout Wrapped in Grape Leaves	685	48.9	15.6	37.4	3.6	585
Provençal Lamb	557	29.3	22.1	26.5	1.1	652	Turkey Steaks with Hummus	311	38.7	3.3	12.1	4.7	418
Quesadillas	721	22.6	17.2	33.1	47.7	1387	Turkey Burgers	404	41.0	1.0	5.2	46.0	1512
Rattlesnake Junction Steak	568	70.0	13.7	16.8	2.4	643	Turkey Sausages	320	26.2	5.9	9.6	19.8	945
Red Chili Aioli	260	0.9	4.4	24.7	0.7	345	Tuscan Chicken	631	64.6	7.8	32.2	8.3	1021
Red Onion & Raisin Relish	426	16	4.6	26.9	36.5	217	Tuscan-Style Steak	658	68.4	15.5	27.3	0.1	624
Refried Beans	450	21.4	15.2	22.3	7.8	738	Two-Bean Cheeseburgers	749	30.9	16.2	34.0	48.5	1682
Roasted Bananas	355	5.0	8.2	6.3	57.2	48	Warm Mushroom Salad	275	4	3.6	23.6	4.2	398
Roasted Carrots	135	0.7	7.3	3.2	10.1	417	Watercress, Grapefruit etc. Salad	121	2.2	1.2	6.5	11.3	53
Roasted Green Chili Salsa	95	3.9	1.2	7.1	1.3	300	White Sausages	387	12.8	13.5	14.9	12.7	387
Roasted Peaches	189	2.1	10.2	4.6	12.6	116	Whole Fish from the Greek Islands	1192	92.1	16.9	74.4	0.1	782
Roasted Vegetables Vinaigrette	610	3.7	18.4	43.2	19.8	2394	Wild Mushroom Sauce	557	3.1	36.2	18.1	6.3	418
Rosemary Polenta	312	7.7	15.3	6.8	21.8	629	Yucatecan Turkey	408	73.4	2.5	4.4	13.8	438
Rosemary-garlic Ciabatta	763	17.8	5.2	29.9	100.6	1138	Zesty Pineapple	50	0.4	-	0.3	13.0	19
S'mores	364	5.1	7.8	8.5	52.6	375							
Salmon & Bacon Kebabs	770	46.8	20.6	39.8	5.3	2781							
Salmon Burgers	520	25.4	15.8	26.6	9.9	353							
Salmon with Chermoula	456	35.3	6.3	27.6	2.4	480							
Salsa	32	1.5	0.1	0.3	6.0	399							
Sardinian Lobster	514	15.4	6.8	39.4	10.5	594							
Sausage Selection	870	35.2	22.9	38.3	46.8	2923							
Scallops with Coconut Sauce	429	32.9	21.3	6.0	7.7	2105							
Scallops with Mushroom Sauce	752	32.1	41.4	21.4	6.7	2657							
Seafood with Mango-Pepper Relish	488	53.3	13.9	12.1	9.6	2059							
She-Devil Barbecue Sauce	182	3.2	-	0.5	397	1053							
Skewers of Chicken Livers	770	37.4	30.9	31.5	15.8	2445							
Smoky-Spicy Corn Salad	382	6.0	6.6	22.9	24.8	1330							
Socca	321	13.7	2.4	14.2	31.3	1482							
Sole with Caper and Butter Sauce	263	32.0	9.5	5.4	248	583							

Breakdowns are per serving. All recipes make four servings, unless otherwise indicated in text.

KEY:
KCAL: energy/calories
CARB: carbohydrates calculated in grams
PRO: protein calculated in grams
FAT(s): saturated fat calculated in grams
FAT(u): unsaturated fat calculated in grams
SOD: sodium calculated in milligrams. (Half a teaspoon of salt assumed if no amount given.)

INDEX

ACKNOWLEDGMENTS

Author's appreciation
I would like to thank:
My daughter Leah, for her endless good taste and
patience. My husband Alan McLaughlan for his
enthusiasm, especially when the summer grew hot and
sultry and barbecuing became a way of life.
All those at Dorling Kindersley who have been such a
pleasure to work with: Daphne Razazan, and the
excellent team of Carolyn Ryden, Alexa Stace and Kate
Scott. Photographer Dave King and his hungry dog Bebe.
Home economists Sunil Vijayakar and Nicola Fowler.
Hoops and Mike Lingwood at Outdoor Chef; and Nigel
Slater for locating this terrific barbecue for me.
Friends in tasting: Jon Harford and his mother Janet,
Simon Parkes, Kathleen Griffin, Shirin and the late
Michael Simmons, Trish and Matthew Robinson, Rhian
Parslow, Peter Milne, Jerome Freeman and Sheila
Hannon, Esther Novak and John Chendo, Christine and
Maureen Smith, Oakland BBQ afficianado Rand
Carreaga, Nigel Patrick, Graham Ketteringham,

Amanda Hamilton and Tim Hemmeter, Sandy Waks,
Kamala Friedman, Paula Levine, Paul Richardson, Etty
and Bruce Blackman, Jason Gaber, Sue Redgrave,
Helene and Robin Simpson, the Wight family.
My parents, Caroline and Izzy Smith, Aunt Estelle and
Uncle Sy Opper, and grandmother Sophia Dubowsky,
who all like a good meal.
M. A. Mariner and Michael Bauer, friends and editors at
the *San Francisco Chronicle*, for commissioning the series
on barbecuing that whetted my appetite for the subject.

Dorling Kindersley would like to thank Nicola
Fowler and Sunil Vijayakar for preparing the food; Sarah
Ponder for the artworks; Julia Schurer of Webers and
The Barbecue Shop, Cobham, Surrey, for the loan of
barbecues and other equipment; Lorna Damms and
Jane Middleton for editorial assistance; and Tracey
Clarke for art assistance.